God Is Always Good:
Cassidy's Story

J. Cameron Fraser
and
Sonya M. Taekema

He lifted me out of the slimy pit, out of the mud and mire; he set my feet on a rock and gave me a firm place to stand. He put a new song in my mouth, a hymn of praise to our God
(Psalm 40:2-3, NIV).

In Psalm 40, David writes about how his experience with God's help during his time of trouble has moved him to praise and others to faith. In its own way, Cassidy's story has the capacity to do the same. It is a story that needs to be told.

Rob vanSpronsen
Principal, Immanuel Christian High School
Lethbridge, Alberta

CASSIDY'S STORY

J. Cameron Fraser and Sonya M. Taekema

GOD

IS ALWAYS GOOD

Guardian
BOOKS

Belleville, Ontario, Canada

GOD IS ALWAYS GOOD

Copyright © 2011, J. Cameron Fraser and Sonya M. Taekema

Cataloguing data available from Library and Archives Canada

The lengthy quotation from John Piper, "Don't Waste Your Cancer," is used by kind permission of www.desiringGod.org. The article is also available as an appendix in John Piper and Justin Taylor (eds.), *Suffering and the Sovereignty of God* (Wheaton, Ill.: Crossway Books, 2006).

ISBN: 978-1-55452-607-9

To order additional copies, visit:
www.essencebookstore.com

For more information, please contact:
www.SoS-Books.com
Available in the U.K. from
www.peterreynoldsbooks.com

Guardian Books is an imprint of *Essence Publishing,* a Christian Book Publisher dedicated to furthering the work of Christ through the written word. For more information, contact:

20 Hanna Court, Belleville, Ontario, Canada K8P 5J2
Phone: 1-800-238-6376 • Fax: (613) 962-3055
Email: info@essence-publishing.com
Web site: www.essence-publishing.com

CONTENTS

PREFACE

This book grew out of a message I (Cameron) gave to my congregation before going to Calgary for a stem cell transplant. The outcome was uncertain at that time, but I wanted to stress that whatever happened, God is always good.

At the service at which I spoke, Sonya's daughter Cassidy (then thirteen) sang a solo. Though unbeknownst to her at the time, she was to have a stem cell transplant of her own a little over a year later. It was of a different kind, allogeneic rather than autologous (see Medical Term Glossary), and for a different condition than mine, but the similarities were enough to give me some understanding of what she was going through.

During the long period of Cassidy's hospitalization, Sonya wrote daily updates, many of which are extracted in the following pages. This makes this book in a real sense Cassidy's story, and we're grateful to her for allowing us to tell it. My story is also told, in briefer form, only by way of introduction to place both stories in the context of God's providential care and goodness at all times. I also provide some concluding thoughts on the same subject as it relates to human suffering. I won't be offended if readers skip what I have written and focus instead on Cassidy's gripping story as told by her mother!

But the ultimate purpose of this book is not so much to

tell either Cassidy's or my story as it is to tell the story of God's providential care. To that end, I hope and pray the theological reflections offered may be of some help. Most of what I have written, and an abbreviated version of Sonya's contribution, have been previously published in successive issues (January/February, March/April, May/June 2010) of the *APC News*, the official publication of the Scottish-based Associated Presbyterian Churches.

Sonya and I are both thankful to our respective spouses and families for their support during the entire period covered in this book, as well as for their encouragement in the writing process. I am grateful to my sister Elizabeth, who came from Scotland to stay with me in Calgary at one crucial time. Thanks to Bob de Moor and Rob vanSpronsen for reading the original manuscript and making several helpful suggestions, some (but not all) of which were acted on. They, of course, are in no way responsible for any infelicities that remain. Robin Aulis also read my contributions and interacted helpfully with them, clarifying one point in particular.

Sincere and humble thanks is extended to all the nurses and doctors who often go well beyond the call of duty in caring for their patients, Cassidy and myself included. Special thanks are due to Osiris Therapeutics, Inc., Columbia, MD, USA, for their interest, life-saving technology, and financial contribution to this project. Most of all, we give praise and glory to God, remembering that whatever the future holds, he is always good.

INTRODUCTION

"And we know that for those who love God all things work together for good, for those who are called according to his purpose." Romans 8:28 is one of those well-known Scripture verses which has brought comfort to God's people in their suffering. It can also be used in an almost clichéd way to give superficial comfort. It shouldn't be quoted too quickly.

It's important to recognize at least two important qualifications. First, this is not just a general assurance that everything will work out well in the end. It's a promise specifically to those who love God. Second, it's for those who are called according to God's purpose. That purpose, as the next verses point out, goes all the way back to God's eternal plan and all the way forward to the glorification of his people, conforming them to the image of his own Son.

This means, among other things, that when suffering comes to those who love God and are called according to his purpose, it is part of his providential care of his people, preparing them for glory. As Paul writes earlier in verse 18 of the same chapter, *"I consider that the sufferings of this present time are not worth comparing with the glory that is to be revealed to us."*

Suffering, then, is part of what we call the doctrine of providence. I'd like to illustrate this from my own experience and then show how it prepared me to minister to others, especially the family of a teenage girl in my congregation. In doing so, my intention is not to suggest that my sufferings have been especially noteworthy. Many have gone through and continue to go through much more than I have. My hope rather, and that of my co-author, is to illustrate the grace of God in his works of providence.

As a young boy in Scotland, I memorized the Westminster Shorter Catechism, which defines God's works of providence as "his most holy, wise, and powerful preserving and governing all his creatures, and all their actions" (Q & A 11). For the last several years, I have ministered to congregations in Canada of mainly Dutch extraction and have grown to know and love their Heidelberg Catechism. I still believe the Shorter Catechism is the best and most concise summary of biblical doctrine available, but the Heidelberg Catechism's tone is more personal and pastoral.

This is readily seen in the Heidelberg Catechism's Lord's Day 10, Q & A 27 and 28:

Lord's Day 10
Q & A 27
Q. What do you understand by the providence of God?
A. Providence is the almighty and ever present power of God by which he upholds, as with his hand, heaven and earth and all creatures, and so rules them that leaf and blade, rain and drought, fruitful and lean years, food and drink, health and sickness, prosperity and poverty—all things, in fact, come to us not by chance but from his fatherly hand.

Q & A 28

Q. How does the knowledge of God's creation and providence help us?

A. We can be patient when things go against us, thankful when things go well, and for the future we can have good confidence in our faithful God and Father that nothing will separate us from his love. All creatures are so completely in his hand that without his will they can neither move nor be moved.

Lord's Day 10, as it is popularly known (the catechism is divided into fifty-two Lord's Days for teaching and preaching purposes), is a great favourite in the circles in which I minister. It was often quoted to me during my illness. But what I found particularly comforting was the previous Lord's Day 9, dealing with the Fatherhood of God:

Lord's Day 9
Q & A 26
Q. What do you believe when you say, "I believe in God, the Father almighty, creator of heaven and earth"?

A. That the eternal Father of our Lord Jesus Christ, who out of nothing created heaven and earth and everything in them, who still upholds and rules the same by his eternal counsel and providence, is my God and Father, because of Christ his Son. I trust him so much that I do not doubt he will provide whatever I need for body and soul, and he will turn to my good whatever adversity he sends me in this sad world. He is able to do this because he is almighty God; he desires to do this because he is a faithful Father.

That last sentence has become one of my personal favourites: "He is able to do this because he is almighty God; he desires to do this because he is a faithful Father."

Home from Hospital

I was diagnosed with lymphoma (a form of cancer) of the spleen in early 2007. Previously, the intention had been to remove my spleen, but when cancer was discovered during the operation, I was sewn back up, spleen intact, and began a course of six chemotherapy sessions in Lethbridge, Alberta, where I live. After this initial treatment, I had a PET (Positron Emission Tomography) scan in Calgary, which still showed a large growth on my spleen but no evidence of cancer cells.

However, the cancer returned, and so the next step was an autologous stem cell transplant. This means that some of my stem cells were removed for safekeeping while I had high-dose chemotherapy, which had the side effect of destroying my bone marrow. Then the stem cells were reintroduced to regenerate the bone marrow. The procedure was given a 50 percent chance of success. This was followed by radiation in the spring of 2008, and I returned to part-time and then full-time work at the beginning of 2009.

A member of my congregation loaned me a very inter-esting book by David Jeremiah, a prominent pastor in California who hosts a radio and TV program called *Turning Point*. The book is called *A Bend in the Road*,[1] and it's mainly a biblical study of suffering, largely from the psalms. It includes the stories of a number of people who have suffered in various ways. But it begins and ends with his own story. At the age of fifty-three, he was diagnosed with a lymphoma of the spleen. A decision was made to operate, but while the operation was in progress, the doctors decided not to take the spleen out as the cancer had not spread as much as they'd thought. This was followed by chemotherapy, which seemed to take care of the problem, at least in the short term. But four years later, the cancer came back, this time in the neck, and David Jeremiah underwent a stem cell trans-plant. This was in 1998-1999, and he is still preaching today.

What struck me about Pastor Jeremiah's experience was the similarities it had to my own. He was fifty-three when he was diagnosed; I was fifty-two. We both underwent surgery to remove the spleen, but in both cases a decision was made not to continue, although for different reasons—his because the cancer had not spread too much, mine because cancer was discovered for the first time. He underwent a stem cell transplant four years after his initial treatment; I did so within a year. His was successful; the results of mine appear to be at present.

After introducing his own story and before getting into the psalms, David Jeremiah discusses two passages of Scripture that have meant a lot to me. The first is 2 Corinthians 12:7-12, which records Paul three times pleading for his thorn in the flesh to be removed, only to receive this wonderful assurance: "*My grace is sufficient for you, for my strength is made perfect in weakness."* So Paul concludes, *"Therefore most gladly I will rather boast in my infirmities, that the power of Christ may rest upon me. Therefore I take pleasure in infirmities, in reproaches, in needs, in persecutions, in distresses, for Christ's sake. For when I am weak, then I am strong"* (NKJV). What extraordinary peace, even joy, this amazing statement offers sufferers! As Ajith Fernando reminds us in another context of suffering, "In 18 different New Testament passages, suffering and joy appear together. In fact suffering is often the cause for joy (Rom. 5:3-5; Col 1:24; James 1:2-3)."[2]

The second passage is Hebrews 12:5-11, which speaks of God disciplining us as sons, assuring us that it is an evidence of his love, painful at the time, but producing *"the peaceable fruit of righteousness"* (NKJV). This doesn't mean that suffering is always a form of discipline. It does mean that we should at least be open to the possibility that God may be working through it to make us the kind of trusting and loving children we ought to be yet might not be if life were too good and we were left to go our own way as we please. As C.S. Lewis famously put it, "God whispers to us in our pleasures, speaks to us in our conscience, but shouts in our pains: It is His megaphone to rouse a deaf world."[3]

A friend wrote to me with a helpful quotation from William Huntington, an English preacher and writer of the past, that included this, which really expresses well my heart's desire: "God hath chosen us in the furnace of affliction, and in affliction he will make his choice of us known." This really is another way of expressing the truth of Hebrews 12:5.

Of course, that doesn't make it easy. Back in the summer of 2007, after my initial PET scan, when I was told that the doctors simply wanted to monitor my condition without any further treatment, I went into a panic and suffered acute anxiety. I wondered how long my wife and I could afford to live on disability payments, whether we should sell our house, if I should simply resign and go on unemployment benefits. These may seem like extreme reactions, and they were—not the kind any Christian should have, much less a pastor who teaches others not to be anxious, as Jesus commanded. At the time I seriously wondered if I could ever preach again. How could I tell others to trust God in a way that I was obviously failing to do?

I received some help from a book of letters by C. John (Jack) Miller called *The Heart of A Servant Leader.* When I was a student at Westminster Theological Seminary in the late 1970s, Jack Miller taught practical theology there and was founding pastor of New Life Presbyterian Church. He later founded World Harvest Mission, which he served as director until his death in 1996. Jack died in Spain after open heart surgery, but he had earlier suffered from lymphoma.

Jack Miller was one of the brightest, most positive, cheerful Christians I have known. Yet he could write in one letter to an AIDS sufferer:

> Consider my cancer or your AIDS. Each person's suffering is unique, but I think I have some feel for what you are going through. No outsider can understand how powerful is the impulse just to lie down and quit—or to give in to fear and despair when you hear the word "cancer" or "AIDS."
>
> For me the month of October in 1987 was a time of heavy-duty anxiety. Happiness? There seemed to be no place for it. The onset of lymphoma really branded my mind so that my emotions were sensitized, even

sometimes dominated, by the whole experience. On the one level, I was easily moved to fear by any fever, tightness of my belt through adding a little weight, or any feeling of unusual tiredness. You may know these are all symptoms of lymphoma—and of a thousand other things. On a deeper level, there was the haunting question of God's dependability, my security in Him. My troubling question was, "If He let me have lymphoma, what is coming next?" And will He permit it to come back?[4]

If Jack Miller of all people could have such thoughts, surely so could I!

Those who tried to help me during this time assured me that I would be able to relate better to the anxieties as well as the physical sufferings of my congregants. The next section of this book will tell the story of one young such sufferer.

PART ONE

My baby's due date was August 2 1994, but because my twenty-three-month-old daughter Kali's birth had been postponed by seventeen days, I wasn't expecting a timely delivery the second time around. So when I experienced the urge to push while at home on the 3rd of August, I was completely shocked—and unprepared.

After a panicked drive to Lethbridge[5] and a brief visit to the delivery room, Dave's and my second daughter was born. She was absolutely perfect, weighing in at the average seven pounds, twelve ounces. We named her Cassidy Rae.

Nursing Cassidy was a struggle, because she would need to be held with her head at a peculiar angle and she would quickly become disinterested. After a two-day layover in the hospital, she and I were able to return home. The feeding issue continued to be a problem at home. She always seemed to be hungry and cried all the time, sleeping little. Concerned something was wrong, I took her to the family doctor on more than one occasion, just to be sure. Her weight, due to the hourly feeds, was increasing nicely, and all other developmental targets were being met. There were no glaring issues—Cassidy was simply an incredibly fussy baby.

She also had very narrow nasal passages and a chronically stuffy nose. Babies typically don't learn to breathe through their mouths until between four and six months of age, but Cassidy, through sheer necessity, started to at six weeks. She first rolled over at about the same time, also due to the struggle with breathing. She slept only an hour at a time at best, drank sips off and on for the next thirty minutes, and cried the rest of the time. (This was very frustrating for me, particularly because I also had a toddler to care for.) Yet she continued to grow.

At two and a half months of age, she received her vaccinations. The following day I noticed she wasn't quite herself—she was actually sleeping and quite lethargic. I called the doctor, who insisted she be seen immediately. I was convinced it was a reaction to the vaccinations but dropped Kali off with my parents and drove the half hour to Lethbridge with Cassidy.

When I arrived at the medical clinic, my baby could barely be roused. The doctor took one look at her and told me that Cassidy needed to be seen by a paediatrician. He wrote up a series of tests he wanted her to undergo, called the specialist, and told me to meet the paediatrician at the emergency room at the city's hospital. It was then that I knew things could be very wrong!

Upon our arrival at the hospital, Cassidy was immediately rushed into a room, and blood was drawn for a multitude of tests. The medical staff also decided to do a spinal tap. I left the room during the procedure on the advice of a nurse but needn't have, for Cassidy did not wake. She was a very sick baby! A marvellous paediatrician, Dr. Khalid Aziz (whom I grew very fond of and dependent upon), then came to talk to me. Dr. Aziz told me that there were some anomalies with Cassidy's white cell count, and he was going to try and find the cause. However, at this point she had no neutrophils and was likely suffering from a serious infection, so a treatment with broad-spectrum intravenous antibiotics was initiated. Cassidy was then admitted to the paediatrics unit. (I later learned that had I waited another 12 hours to have her seen by doctors, she would likely not have survived.)

Cassidy's skin was translucent—a pale blue hue. Her eyes and face were puffy and her temperature high, with little relief offered from Tylenol. There was little difference between her sleeping and waking moments but for the fact that she would want to drink, but then only small sips at a time. She was poked and prodded, had numerous tests performed on her, and was being infused with antibiotics and fluids around the clock. We prayed fervently that the drugs would be effective and that her neutrophils would recover to normal levels as her infection resolved. We realized that she had been fighting this her whole young life and that the fight had taken all her energy. I felt real guilt for having been so frustrated with her when all along she had been struggling to stay alive. And I hoped that as she experienced physical well-being she would also be more content.

A couple of weeks into her treatment, I came down the hall one morning to her room. She was sitting in the hallway in a stroller, and she turned, looked at me, and the most beautiful smile lit up her face! This was the spirit of the child I loved! It was at that moment that true bonding between mother and daughter began.

Shortly thereafter we were sent to Calgary to have Cassidy undergo diagnostic tests and treatments at the Alberta Children's Hospital. It was at this time that our worst fears were realized—she indeed did have a very rare disorder, severe chronic congenital neutropenia, also known as Kostmann's syndrome. This meant that her bone marrow produced no neutrophils, which are the body's main defence against bacterial infection. There were two options presented to us: a highly risky bone marrow transplant, which she had a 50 percent chance of surviving; or a drug therapy consisting of daily injections of a granulocyte-colony stimulating factor (G-CSF), which had potential long-term side effects but would hopefully boost the production of white cells and at least provide some added protection. (This drug had only been approved for use in Alberta three years prior.) The latter was the best option for a relatively normal life, and so the daily injections began. There was a chance the drug wouldn't work, in which case a transplant would be the only option.

It took six agonizing days, but finally there were signs of neutrophils—"SuperNeuts" we called them—and eventually we returned home.

The next five years were stressful ones, with many trips to the emergency room, countless blood tests and antibiotic treatments, numerous admissions to the local paediatrics ward, and a few stays at the Alberta Children's Hospital. We had to find out through trial and error which physical, dietary, and medical restrictions were necessary to protect Cassidy and about which we could relax. This was not easy to do when any wrong decision could result in a life-threatening infection, of which she suffered many. But she always recovered, thank God.

The night before Cassidy's first day of school in 1999, she presented with a low-grade fever (anything above 38 degrees centigrade necessitated a trip to the emergency room). I remember feeling her hot forehead beneath my hand as she slept. A wave of disappointment washed over me as I realized, yet again, how far removed from normal

Cassidy's life had become. While I touched her, I prayed that God would remove the fever so that she could enjoy this important milestone. As I prayed, her fever broke.

Her elementary school years were relatively healthy. Though she was ill and hospitalized occasionally, we could really feel God's protection over her as she participated as much as possible in school events and field trips—some of which were risky but important to her development. She had an enlarged spleen as a result of her disease, so contact sports had to be avoided. She suffered somewhat from asthma, particularly following a cold; she developed eczema; she had chronic inflammation of her tonsils, so required a tonsillectomy; she had an anaphylactic reaction to a bug bite; and always there were concerns about infections, but God shielded her from many of the complications that, for her, could have been deadly. In grade 4, she even received recognition for perfect attendance! She was definitely living a life we had never dreamed would be possible for her.

Her junior high school years proved to be quite similar and provided many opportunities to lead the life of an ordinary student. The most significant opportunity came when one winter we discovered kidney-protectors used by lacrosse players. Cassidy would be able to use this piece of equipment to shield her enlarged spleen. This meant that many of the sports that had been off-limits to her could now be played. My sweet girl cried tears of happiness when she realized the significance of this simple gift. She could now play competitive badminton and be able to take part in all the sports in gym class. She's quite the athletic girl, so this was pure joy for her!

She is also very creative and is often happiest fabricating intricate models out of scraps and pieces of whatever she finds. She loves to sing and has blessed us numerous times with solos in church, at school concerts, and during services at senior citizens' homes. But most importantly, she has faith I can only hope to be gifted with. She speaks of an instance early on when she woke to find an angel standing at the foot of her bed, which assured her of God's presence and protection, and her eyes light up in the telling.

Over the course of the past two years, however, Cassidy's faith has been tested beyond anything I could imagine at her age. In January of 2008, she went for a routine blood test. The results showed, for the first time in her life, a completely normal blood count! Of course we had the test redone, just to be sure, but over and over again they showed normal neutrophil counts.

We were ecstatic and quickly shared the great news, with praises to God coming first. We gradually reduced the dosage of G-CSF, and her counts remained in the normal range. We got down to 0.1 ml/day, and though she still appeared to need that small amount to keep the levels up, it was miraculous! Her paediatrician in Lethbridge, Dr. Maya Harilal, kept a close eye on her and discovered over repeated examinations that the swelling of her spleen had also decreased substantially. This meant that, though still needing to be cautious, Cassidy had more freedom of activity and movement than she'd ever experienced before.

Her haematologist in Calgary called, and though an annual bone marrow biopsy had been done in October (routine to watch out for any mutations, which can occur both as a result of the disease and as a side-effect of the G-CSF), the doctor wanted to do another one, just to see what was causing the changes to the blood counts. Reluctantly, we agreed. We really wanted Cassidy to enjoy her new-found freedom and not continue to be poked and prodded but knew the doctors needed to be cautious as well. So in early July, she went in. All went well, there were no complications, and preliminary results showed no abnormalities.

Life went on as normal. In late August we met up with family in British Columbia for a camping holiday. We had a mostly fabulous time, minus some weather issues.

One day I was at the local laundromat when my cell-phone rang. I answered, and it was the haematologist in Calgary informing me that because of some anomalies that had shown up on the biopsy, she needed us to come up to Calgary—the sooner the better, but to enjoy our holiday first. Oh, and Cassidy had to discontinue the G-CSF completely, and immediately.

I was so glad I was alone at that moment. The fear that had gnawed at me throughout Cassidy's life now roared and bared its ugly teeth. Before I could panic, however, the words, "Did I not say I would take care of you?" entered my mind. Immediately I was calmed, and I phoned my husband, Dave, to come meet me. We discussed what had transpired, cried and prayed together, and went back to the girls.

We told them that the doctor from Calgary had called, and because of some test results Cassidy had to stop her injections. We didn't share further, because it was important for Kali and Cassidy to stay innocent and have carefree fun as long as possible. The following night we stayed in a very posh hotel, uncertain when our next chance would be to enjoy a vacation together.

On August 28 we headed to Calgary. Once there, we were informed that Cassidy's chromosomes had mutated and if untreated would develop into acute myelogenous leukemia, which is terribly difficult to cure. The technical name for her new disease was monosomy 7. Two options were presented to us: to wait and see, which was highly risky, or a stem cell transplant. Another bone marrow biopsy was performed to track the progression of the monosomy 7, but we opted to pursue a transplant.

Our world fell apart! Everything had been going so well, it felt like the rug had been pulled out from under us.

And yet, in the midst of this turmoil, there emerged the simple but profound belief that this was how Cassidy would finally experience the miracle of complete healing and have a disease-free body. And that's the hope we clung to as we moved forward to transplant. Cassidy never worried—she had a God-given peace all the way through.

We moved forward to transplant rather quickly. No one in our immediate family was a match, so the bone marrow transplant team started actively searching for a donor in September of 2008, a process that takes anywhere from a few months to a year. On November 5, just two months later, we were informed that they had found a perfect match! However, we were quickly confronted with having to make a big decision.

Shortly after finding a donor match, we received a call from the haematologist who informed us that the monosomy 7 had regressed. We needed to decide once again whether a transplant was truly the best option. We looked back on all that had transpired to this point—the way God had guided us and the doctors. Anchored in faith that God was definitely at work, we told the doctors to continue moving forward with the transplant. From there, we had several more appointments in Calgary to prepare for trans-plant (including another bone marrow biopsy), and on December 14 Cassidy was admitted to the oncology unit at the Alberta Children's Hospital. We knew going in that Cassidy (and I as well) would have to remain in Calgary (a two and a half hour drive from home) for a minimum 100 days post-transplant.

There are many risks associated with stem cell transplants, but the technology has advanced tenfold since Cassidy was a baby, and we really felt God had protected her all these years to get her to this point. Everything leading up to transplant worked so smoothly, it was impossible not to see God's hand in it. As further evidence of this, we were told that Cassidy's latest biopsy showed a rapid progression of her disease. We knew then with absolute certainty we had made the right choice.

Alberta Children's Hospital

Cassidy went through a week of chemotherapy, to which she didn't react too badly. On December 23 she received the cells that would change so much of her life. All went well but for a fever in the middle of the night. She was put on antibiotics just to be safe, but it ended up being a simple post-transplant reaction, and she had no fevers afterward.

There were no huge issues after that point—at least nothing unexpected—and she recovered quite well. Mucositis (a painful inflammation and ulceration of the mucous membranes lining the digestive tract) became an issue briefly, but she continued to eat in spite of it, thanks in part to morphine. She also needed one blood transfusion just to help boost her haemoglobin.

On January 6 we were given the news that, for the first time in her life, Cassidy's marrow was making its own adult neutrophils—without the aid of G-CSF! This meant that the marrow was indeed grafting. And things just continued to get better from there. Her mucositis eased, she was able to take all her medications orally, she was eating enough that her IV (intravenous) nutrition could be safely removed, and she sped right along to discharge, which was the 17th of January, 2009.

Cassidy and I moved into the Ronald McDonald House, which is in close proximity to the Alberta Children's Hospital. Despite their busyness at home and their own stresses, Dave and Kali were able to join us most weekends. The following months had their ups and downs, but Cassidy remained healthy and strong. Around us there were so many families going through their own trials, and we couldn't help but feel extraordinarily blessed that she was doing so incredibly well—so well, in fact, that we were able to go home on April 1, day 99. Thank you, Jesus!

The adjustment to being home was not an easy one, though Cassidy was most enthusiastic about seeing her friends outside of school. She was still much too immuno-suppressed to be out in public, and she was restricted in what foods she could eat, so that was a bit challenging for her. As the week progressed, though, it became easier for both of us.

Until the 8th of April, when she woke up with a rash.

PART TWO

Initially I thought the rash was due to some jewellery Cassidy had been wearing overnight, but when it didn't ease and started to spread, I called the oncologist in Calgary. The bone marrow transplant team member I spoke to advised us to come up the next day, as Good Friday was on the 10th, and she didn't want us to wait past the long weekend. So, with fear and trepidation, we made the return trip to the place that had been our home for many months.

Several doctors came to examine Cassidy. They were looking to rule out graft versus host disease (GVHD), a potential complication of stem cell transplants in which the newly transplanted cells attack the recipient's body. The rash's appearance and presentation were definitely not classic GVHD, but the doctors set up an emergency appointment with a dermatologist, just to be sure. The dermatologist was more certain it was GVHD, but a very mild case, which, he assured us, was not a cause for great concern. He sent us home with a prescription for topical steroid creams, and we left Calgary once again for Lethbridge.

On Easter morning however, it was apparent that Cassidy's condition was not improving, and possibly deteriorating. She had developed vomiting and diarrhea, which are potential symptoms of GVHD. So, after again talking with the oncologist in Calgary, we decided to make our way back up to the Alberta Children's Hospital.

Cassidy's Easter message

Upon admission, it was obvious that Cassidy was dehydrated, so immediately the staff started to infuse her with fluids. My husband, Dave, and our older daughter, Kali, left for home shortly thereafter, as he had work and she had school the next day. After all, we felt our stay would be a brief one—get the fluids in her, get the diarrhea and vomiting under control, and we'd be on our way. Little did we know!

The search was on to determine what was causing the symptoms Cassidy was experiencing. We had gastrointestinal doctors surmising about possible viral infections, doctors from oncology looking closely at the GVHD possibility, and doctors from infectious diseases looking at the possibility of a parasite. An agreement was finally made; a suspected parasite in her stool and named "Wall-e" by the doctors was possibly responsible for some of Cassidy's symptoms, but not for all of them. Her rash and diarrhea intensified, so it was decided to start her on steroids to treat GVHD and also a treatment to eradicate the parasite. In the end, "Wall-e's" true identity was never discovered, as the sample was lost in the laboratory and was never studied!

The symptoms did not improve and, indeed, worsened. On the 16th of April, after about a week without the benefit of any food, intravenous nutrition was begun. The same day it was decided—rather suddenly—that an endoscopy and biopsy of the gut needed to be performed. This was terrifying for my girl, whose body had already turned against her. How much more would she have to endure?

The endoscopy was mostly successful but for a bit of bleeding afterwards. And the results showed conclusively that GVHD was the main cause of Cassidy's symptoms. In fact, the GVHD was categorized as grade 4 of the gut—the worst possible but for the fact the liver wasn't affected.

After the scope and biopsy, Cassidy started to expel blood, and blood only, through her stool and vomit—this was terrifying! The doctors continued the standard protocol of treating her with steroids and immunosuppressants, but it had little to no effect on her condition. The pain she was experiencing was certainly heart- and gut-wrenching—both for us and her.

This part of the journey was extremely difficult for Cassidy. She usually has a very good attitude about her illnesses and their treatments. Even going in to transplant she was the least worried of us all! I think the uncertainty on the part of the doctors, the lack of progress in healing, and the general lack of diagnosis and treatment really affected her spirit. Not the positive girl I was used to, so this was very trying for me in that respect as well. Seeing her suffer and look at me wordlessly made me an emotional wreck.

On the evening of April 19, in the hope of healing her badly damaged intestine and stomach linings, it was decided to start Cassidy on a drug typically used for Crohn's patients. However, her condition was so grave and the effectiveness of this drug so questionable, the doctors advised Dave to stay for the next few days. Kali went home to stay with family friends, as sitting around waiting and watching was not what we considered to be in her best interests.

On April 20, the doctors told us about a new therapy undergoing clinical trials in the United States. It takes adult mesenchymal stem cells, and after being infused into the patient, these cells are to go to sites of inflammation, resolve the inflammation, and proceed to rebuild injured tissues. (In Cassidy's case, the entire lining of her stomach and intestines needed to be regenerated.) However, this therapy is not available in Canada, but the doctors were hoping to get permission on compassionate grounds to use it on Cassidy.

This was the best news we had heard yet, for obviously other methods of treatment were not working, and Cassidy was getting sicker and frailer, and her pain was increasing. We knew something had to be done and finally had some hope to hold on to.

The doctors worked around the clock, filling out forms, talking to officials, until April 22, when they gained approval from Health Canada, the university and hospital boards, and Osiris Therapeutics Inc. (the pharmaceutical company) to obtain the cells for Cassidy's treatment. All involved realized this was really her last option for healing and were more than co-operative.

That day Cassidy, for the first time, requested morphine for her pain. Her pain was getting too much for her tired body to fight. And that night she finally was able to get some sleep.

The afternoon of the 24th was the first of the mesenchymal stem cell infusions. The plan was to infuse these cells twice a week for four weeks. The cells worked as hoped, but not as quickly as we would have liked, so four more infusions over four weeks were added.

Mesenchymal Stem Cells

The remaining part of this story will be told through extracts from updates I wrote to friends and family on a daily basis. The use of commonly used abbreviations and conversational language (including occasional slang) is intentionally preserved:

April 29: Today was definitely a day of ups and downs. Cassidy had a relatively good night, but for a nurse who tended to pace the room while waiting for the IV pump to beep off (???!!!). Cassidy woke around 9 a.m., watched some

Cosby Show—and then a group of three walked into the room.

Now, Cassidy *hates* it when there is more than one person talking to her, examining her, or asking things of her at one time. So already her guard was up. The doctor in the group proceeded to tell her that she will have to undergo another surgery to insert yet another central line into her. The Broviac that she has is working perfectly, but they need more access than it offers, as there are so many drugs and fluids that they have to give her in a day and it just isn't happening optimally right now. So, it looks like they'll be adding one with two lumens, or IV access tubes, inserted into a vein in her arm sometime this week. She's not happy about this at all! On the plus side, they will be able to give her nutrition and lipids more consistently, so weight loss may no longer be an issue. The plan is also to give her a morphine pump so she'll have better pain control. But, though understandable and necessary, it pretty much blows. Still, it could be worse.

She was also fairly disappointed when she went to the bathroom this morning and once again (after forty-eight hours of none) passed blood in her stool. Not what she, nor I, was hoping for. But the docs impressed on us once again that it will take serious time for the intestines and stomach to heal. So, I guess we need another lesson in patience?

Later on we spent serious time watching some TV, talking to Dave and Kali on the phone, all between the bathroom trips, IV infusions, bathroom trips, morphine doses, bathroom trips, visits from docs and nurses, waiting for the time it was okay for another morphine dose...

We then closed the night with a reading from Psalm 30. I've read it many times before, but a friend drew my attention back to it, and it really resonated with both Cassidy and me. Was a great way to end a topsy-turvy day!

April 30: What started out as a day where Cassidy was relatively chipper, nothing major was going to occur, and the mood was almost bright, turned into one of frustration, anger, and tears on the part of my beloved daughter.

She was up at 8:30 a.m., had an infusion of albumin, and had settled down nicely in her bed with the remote control close at hand. Dr. Lewis came in and examined her. While concerned about her pain level and the occasional presence of blood in her stool, he was positive about the rapid fading of her rash and her demeanour in general. Time and patience are the two major keys to her recovery, and he impressed on her to keep her fighting spirit. And to pray that the mesenchymal stem cells would do the rest. So, though no magic cure was being offered, it wasn't devastating news, anyway. We'll take what we can get.

Tomorrow it was planned to have another infusion of the cells and the surgery to insert another central line. Though not pleased with this, Cassidy had resigned herself to accept it and just wanted to enjoy today.

Then docs came in and told her that the surgery would happen today and that they would have to put the PICC line in her right arm, so as not to put added stress on the vessel on the left side where the Broviac is. Well, she was understandably upset, to say the least. "Why can't I just have one good day?" At 5:30 p.m., she went into surgery, unaware that if the arm central line didn't work they'd have to put another Broviac in her chest. To say I was nervous was an understatement, for that would have been even more devastating to her. Thankfully, when they wheeled her back in the room at 7:00 p.m., the doc said everything went fine, and because of new technology available to them they found a great vein deep in the arm that worked fantastically.

This evening has been a challenge. Cassidy's now on a morphine pump, so she has a bit more control over the pain, but it's not giving her the good hit she's used to at night, and she's not getting the sleepy feeling she's been enjoying as of late. Hopefully she'll get the hang of it and will realize the benefits outweigh any negatives. She's been a very angry girl tonight, though. Ticked at how she's become even less mobile, ticked at even more pain due to the surgery, ticked at the fact it now takes her longer to get to the bathroom...generally ticked. I was also getting to the end of my rope. So hard to see your kid upset, understand why she's upset, but be powerless to do anything about it.

But then she broke down. Cried a bit. Fell into my arms and sobbed. And then everything got a bit better. She's now lying in bed, waiting for the morphine to do something, waiting for sleep to come, but generally content. Obviously, though not making her sleepy, the drugs are taking the edge off the pain, which really is a great thing.

The kid's been through so much, my heart cries for her, and yet so much of the time I'm unable to do anything to help. Except love her unconditionally, and I guess for now that will have to be enough.

Tomorrow night Dave and Kali will be coming up, so Dave will take a couple of night shifts here and I'll get to spend some much-needed time with my other daughter, who's been suffering through all this, too. Pray that we will have a good weekend together and that things will settle down here and Cassidy will start showing signs of real improvement, and hopefully sooner than the doctors expect (please God??!!!) I think we've had enough lessons in patience for now.

May 1: Today was an all right day overall. It was busy, because Cassidy had her third infusion of the MSCs, another infusion of albumin, more Benadryl, and really a lot more infusions over all, due to the fact that she now has four lumens to be used. She's also getting used to the morphine pump.

Two doctors and a nurse practitioner came in this morning to examine Cassidy. They are "encouraged" by a lower stool output yesterday, and by the changed form of the blood that is present in it. Any time doctors say they're encouraged (especially around here) is a cause for (guarded) celebration. And *always* thanks to God!

Cassidy also had a visit from the resident chaplain today. He just came in casually, introduced his mandolin to her, chatted about that, and played some snappy little tunes. She quite enjoyed it, especially the fact that he talked to her "normal." The girl is so tired of people asking how she's feeling, how she rates her pain, where the pain is, how she is coping...She just needed some normal, non-medical, easy conversation, and thankfully Marcel provided that.

Cassidy had a pretty good day! Her stool output was down by a whole litre over the average from earlier this week, so that's *fantastic*!!! Her pain was also either better managed (due to the morphine pump) or lessened. She didn't seem as uncomfortable today. She looked and acted brighter through most of the day, but was really tuckered tonight. *If* this is a sign of healing, the road will (barring a miracle—which I would welcome wholeheartedly!) still be a very long one, as all the lining in her intestines will have to rebuild, and until that's done she will still be unable to take anything by mouth. IV only! And she won't be able to leave the hospital until she can be IV-free. So please pray that healing continues, that it goes more quickly than the doctors expect (I think this would be an anomaly they would welcome!), and that in the meantime she remains free from any viral, bacterial, or fungal infections, as she has no way of fighting these at this point.

Long road ahead, but one I'm willing to travel, especially if it means Cassidy will once again be whole and healthy.

May 6: Cassidy's urine tested positive for the adenovirus. This is a virus that can take many different forms, and bladder bleeding is one of them. She is now going to have her stool retested for it, as well as her blood. Thankfully, at this point she has no other symptoms, so *please pray* that this remains the case. She will likely be starting on an antiviral med to nip it in the bud, so *please pray* that it works and that she suffers no side effects from it!

Due to the extended period of bleeding (intestinal and now bladder), her haemoglobin has dropped, and she will be getting a blood transfusion this afternoon.

All this has come as a bit of a blow to all of us, but particularly Cassidy. *Please pray* that we all remain positive, enjoy the little things each day, and continue to count our blessings. Right now she is crafting and has been playing bingo, so that's a blessing in and of itself.

May 8: Friday was a good day for Cassidy. She got the Benadryl and stem cell infusion out of the way in the morning, and by this afternoon she was sitting up in bed painting picture frames. She stuck to this for a good couple of hours, so that was a very positive thing. She was bright, smiling and talkative. She was Cassidy.

At 9 this evening I got a call from her doctor (who was at home). He called to let me know that the tests taken earlier this week revealed that the adenovirus was also in her blood. This is not a good thing, particularly because she is so immunosuppressed. However, the fact that she has no symptoms but the bladder bleeding gives us hope that it has been caught early.

So, once again, the doctors were on the phone with Health Canada and filing the proper paperwork, getting approval for her to use a new antiviral drug that should erad-icate this virus. It should also take care of a number of other viruses, in case she also has those hiding inside. There are potential risks, however, but they have another drug that they prescribe alongside that will counter those effects. So they are definitely giving her the best of chances.

We received the approval late this evening. Right now Cassidy is gagging down the other med (which has to be taken orally and is not pleasant—not what she envisioned her first "food" in four weeks to be!), and the first infusion of the approved antiviral med will be sometime in the wee hours of this morning. She will also be highly hydrated, so, once again, frequent visits to the bathroom will be inter-rupting the night.

Though devastating news once again, the fact that she had the bladder bleeding that triggered the further testing was (in retrospect) a blessing of sorts. At least this allowed the docs to catch the virus in the blood before she became symptomatic, hopefully nipping it in the bud before it has a chance to do any serious damage.

I once again give thanks for highly dedicated doctors and

nurses who work diligently to get Cassidy well and try to keep her that way...I also tip my hat to Cassidy herself, who, though down, has never given up and shows great courage in the face of adversity. She amazes me, and is more evidence of God's grace.

May 11: This was not a great day...things kind of stalled and even rolled back a bit. Cassidy's energy level was down and her pain level up. This may be due to an adjustment to one of her meds, which was again readjusted later today. Please pray this is all it was and that tomorrow will be a brighter day all around.

She is really trying to stay positive, but it's so hard when the body doesn't play along. It's been such a long road for her, and really, it's a testament to her faith and general attitude that she hasn't fallen into a pit of self-pity. I'm sure I would have caved in a long time ago.

There still are small signs of improvement, which made today's turn of events puzzling and disconcerting. Cassidy's stool is changing form a bit, and we hope for the better. There is no longer any visible blood in the urine (not to say that there isn't any microscopic). Her weight has again stabilized. So much to thank God for! So much more to pray for...*please* keep praying that the One with *all* the Power blesses us soon with real and permanent healing. That's really all we need.

May 16: Yesterday Cassidy had her seventh infusion of the MSCs, and all went well. Next Tuesday's infusion was to be the last, but the doctors believe they are indeed making a difference and want to continue the infusions for a while longer. So that is what we'll do—whatever helps.

Today she had her second dose of the antiviral med prescribed for the adenovirus. She will probably be tested again this week for that, to see if that med needs to be continued. Hopefully the clots in the urine will ease up soon.

May 20: Just a quick note tonight to let you know we're all doing okay. Our evening was pleasant, though Cassidy was pretty tired again throughout the day, still experiencing belly discomfort. The doctors explained it could be the "withdrawal" from the morphine, or it could be that because of the lower dose of morphine the muscles in her gut are no longer as paralyzed—waking up, stretching, and aching from their long rest. So let's hope and pray that is what it is. There are more bowel sounds, so that is a good sign.

Tomorrow around 1:30 p.m., Cassidy will be getting a CT scan of her abdomen. Please pray that they find (remarkable) improvement! After that, Cassidy's doctors along with the GI (gastrointestinal) docs will be discussing where to go and what to do from here. So hopefully what they see on the scan will make them discuss steps forward!

So *please* pray this to be the case! We've been here now for thirty-eight days, and it's been forty-one or forty-two since she's had a meal. Progress would be so very sweet...for all of us, but especially for Cassidy. Good news would be the *best* medicine!

May 24: Cassidy had a good day yesterday and was able to enjoy the companionship of her dad and sister. So, yes, we've had a couple of mostly positive days, and for that we rejoice and are grateful! However, as anyone following our story can attest to, this does not mean she's out of the woods or that there will be no more hurdles. She still has grade 4 GVHD of the gut, she still has the adenovirus, and she is still highly immunosuppressed. I don't mean to sound ungrateful or pessimistic, but this is the reality, and my main purpose in writing you these updates is to paint you an honest picture of what is going on, and to allow those of you who pray to be specific in your requests.

Tonight I also wanted to spend some time in thanks. Thanks for many things and many people. Our family has been blessed by the generosity of friends, family, colleagues, and strangers, and our hearts are full of gratitude to you all. So, to those who have contributed: time, meals, finances, labour, cards, letters, gifts, rides, e-mails, a place for our dog to stay, help for Kali when she/we needed it, and above all, prayers, *thank you*! It really doesn't seem adequate, but it is most sincere.

May the Lord shower you with his grace, may his favour shine upon you, and may you reap blessings abundant!

May 26: Today I spent a fair bit of time corresponding back and forth with a very wise and kind friend. What a blessing that was! Email and Facebook have truly been godsends for me, because other forms of communication are either difficult or impossible. It is such a gift to be able to converse in a way that still allows me the flexibility of tending to my other responsibilities.

So I count those as blessings one and two.

Dave and Kali are doing well. Dave is very busy with work, Kali with school and such (?), plus tending to the household responsibilities takes time and effort on their part. Thanks to those who provide meals for them, for that is then one less thing for them to have to concern themselves with.

So I count those as blessings three, four, and five.

Cassidy had a reasonably good night. Not as good as the past two, but unremarkable in any negative manner as well. Her haemoglobin, which we were concerned about, seems to be rising on its own, so no transfusions today! Her day was spent very lazily, with a bit of paper art mixed in with television viewing, minimal physio, and infrequent trips to the loo. She was in good spirits for the most part, and her boluses of morphine were rare.

Blessings six, seven, eight, nine, ten, and eleven.

I spent a good portion of my evening in playful banter with friends young and not-so-young on Facebook, which often makes me smile, and just gives a bit of levity to my mood. Cassidy probably thinks her mom is losing it at times when I laugh out loud while looking at a computer screen, but really, those are some of my most sane moments! Good friends are priceless!

Blessings abundant!

Amazing how hard it is to count your blessings because, as a great friend told me, there are so many!

I pray you are as blessed as I am.

May 27: Cassidy was up and crafting for a bit again today, played Wednesday bingo, watched television, and enjoyed a bit of sit-down basketball with a hoop and ball she won at bingo (she's doing physio without realizing it!). All in all, a good day for her!

Another family here experienced the opposite today as their very young son succumbed to the cancer he's been fighting for the past two years. So once again my heart goes out to people who never got to leave here as an intact family. I am so sorry.

This whole experience here—the tangible frailty of life,

the devastating disappointment, the shared grief, and the united joy—is at once precious and painful to me. It truly makes you take a long hard look at your own life and reprioritize. I am no longer sure of who I am or what I want or need out of life, or what I want or need to contribute to this world we live in, and, for me personally, it would be shameful to go through a situation like this and not learn and grow from it.

May 28: This was another good day—continued weaning off meds, more art work done by Cassidy, and fewer complaints from her all around. And that's *with* the morphine drop. Praise the Lord for all this! And please pray that her health continues to improve. It can be slow, but slow progress is much better than any more steps backward or stalls. She mentioned today that she heard her stomach growl, and that she thought she was hungry!!!!!!!

This is indeed progress, but scary at the same time. The doctors told us that they want to be sure they are doing the right thing before they start to introduce food, as they don't want to further injure the gut. They are surmising it might be a couple of weeks yet till she can start ingesting anything. Which in and of itself is understandable, and thankfully Cassidy understands, but there's something else at work here—steroids. And steroids can cause uncontrollable hunger cravings. This could prove to be a nightmare of torture for Cassidy. So please pray it doesn't come to that. It was bad enough she couldn't eat when her body wasn't sending hunger signals. This could be a trial of a new sort.

May 31: Watching my daughter literally fight for her life has changed me. And, like her healing, it's not yet a completed process. I've never before had so much time alone with my own thoughts, both good and bad, and it's created opportunity, welcome or not, for a lot of self-reflection and evaluation. Not all of it is pretty, and I believe that God is using this opportunity to show that to me, and hopefully I will be receptive to the lessons I must learn from it.

So the picture of me that I may have, inadvertently, painted for you through my updates is not complete. What you see on the outside isn't all there is. I feel more flawed than ever and am trying to work through a number of issues pertaining to my life and faith. Sometimes writing the updates is cathartic and really allows me to see things (life, faith, and God) more clearly. Oftentimes I write them to and for myself as much as for all of you. I hope you all can appreciate and understand that. My main intention is the same: to share our story and to bring people to prayer for Cassidy.

June 2: This morning Cassidy woke up to severe nausea, which has lasted all day, but for the anti-nausea med she is now on. What's causing this? Hopefully it's something as simple as hunger and a perpetually empty stomach that's trying to digest something that's not there. Pray that is what it is and not some other problem.

One thing I've experienced, through all of this turmoil in our lives, is an ever-growing distaste for complaints over minutiae. I realize not everyone has experienced the same degree of life-changing circumstances we have, so I try to be understanding and patient in this regard. But to be perfectly honest, I'm finding that harder and harder to do. I read a quote today that illustrates my point better than I could. Hopefully it will cause you to pause—and look up—the next time you want to whine about a trivial matter:

Sometimes it seems like God is difficult to find and impossibly far away. We get so caught up in our small daily duties and irritations that they become the only things that we can focus on. What we forget is that God's love and beauty are all around us, every day, if only we would take the time to look up and see them.[6]

So love those with whom God has blessed you, forgive those who may have been less-than-perfect, laugh at yourself once in a while, and be grateful to God for all the abundance in your life.

June 3: Today was a good news day! Cassidy decided (with her doctor's help) to stop the continuous infusion of morphine. She still has the power to give herself a "hit" when she needs to, but she hasn't needed to much, if at all, today. *Yay*!!! The latest blood test for the adenovirus came out negative, and if it stays that way over the next few weeks, she will be considered to have cleared that hurdle. She will continue the antiviral meds in the meantime. *Yay*!!!

Her doctor also had the privilege of informing us that the GVHD in her gut had gone from grade 4 to grade 2 or 1!!! This is huge, and the best news we've had yet! So what's in store for her now? Well, the doctors are (thankfully) being very cautious, and so will, starting next week, slowly reintroduce food. A digestive system that has had nothing to digest in nearly two months will probably not take very kindly to that, so "slowly" is the operative word here. They will also slowly start weaning her off steroids, and at some point her immunosuppressant. They are also trying to get more MSCs for her, as she has responded so well to this therapy and they don't want to stop it until she no longer has need for it. *Yay*!!!!

So much to give thanks for! Praise God for all good things! The road ahead is still unknown, and all steps forward could lead to new obstacles, but she has conquered so many of them already, so today for that we give thanks.

June 8: Ten millilitres of broth every hour. Is that exciting, or what! Cassidy was a little choked when she heard that was what her "meals" were going to consist of, but thankfully she's old enough to understand why. She was also told that this decision would be revisited daily and, depending on how her body adjusts, additions may be made. So she made the best of it, savouring every last drop, watching the clock for the next hour to pass so she could have more...And every hour on the hour her mother's going to the kitchen, getting the bowl from the fridge, drawing up the requisite amount into an oral syringe, transferring it to a dish, heating it in the microwave for a whole eight seconds, and then bringing it down the (long!) hall to her awaiting princess. Two seconds later it's gone. I spend more energy getting it ready for her than she receives from ingesting it! Oh well, all part of the weight-loss program (mine, that is).

She did well with it, too. No belly pain, no nausea, and no increased stool—the first day went marvellously! Thank you, Lord!

June 9: Praises to our Lord and Saviour! The doctor came in today with great news! Cassidy's GVHD has again been downgraded—this time to grade zero!!!!!!! The relief I felt was physical—immediate headache, neck and back pain—I never knew how tense I was! But the pain is more than welcome when it's in response to such great news!

Food-wise things have changed, too. Because the "test"

yesterday went so well, she can now eat small amounts of broth, sugar-free Jello, water, diet ginger ale, and sugar-free popsicles—pretty well as much as she wants, as long as she listens to her body. The best is just small sips throughout the day, in order to retrain and rebuild the gut. So today she's had about two and a half cups of liquid, and only got sick once (after the popsicle). She "hears" her body very well and doesn't push the eating thing, though she's enjoying it very much! It'll be a very slow process, but we want to take it slowly so we don't risk a relapse. The MSCs are also planned for this Friday—the last in this series—and she will no longer be receiving those unless she needs them again at some point. Pray she won't!

June 12: I'm back in Calgary after being home for two days. Very good, but odd, days. My daughter Kali had a band and choir concert on Wednesday night, which I was privileged to enjoy. It was fabulous, and seeing all the kids again, many of my colleagues, some family, and having the opportunity to see/hear my girl shine was well worth the trip! I was/am a very proud mama! Great, too, was the chance to spend "normal" time with Kali—it's been a very long time! Odd, though, because as I was going about relatively normal business, my other daughter was in hospital. So, whether I'm here or there, there's nothing normal about our life.

Today Cassidy had her (hopefully) last infusion of the MSCs, and Benadryl. And, though much of the day was a wash, she perked up mid-afternoon, and by the time Kali and I arrived (after battling terrible bottleneck traffic), she was in great spirits, and we had a nice evening together as a family.

One thing that we've never been told by Cassidy's doctors, and I've been too afraid to ask, is whether the transplant was successful in removing disease from Cassidy's marrow. I did not want to deal with the possibility that it hadn't while we are still dealing with the GVHD, so I never asked. Dave, however, wasn't quite so timid and asked her doctor today. The doc was shocked that we hadn't heard yet but happily told Dave that the marrow was all clear! Hallelujah! So all we have to concern ourselves with at this time is eliminating the GVHD altogether.

Tonight Dave and Cassidy were so kind and generous as to allow Kali and me one last night together at the RMH. We watched some completely frivolous and ridiculously fun videos together.

Now it's time for some sleep.

I wish you all a blessed weekend. Hold your loved ones close.

June 14: Cassidy's been doing reasonably well with her all-liquid diet, though the novelty has definitely worn off. I do believe the girl would like to try something with more flavour and texture. Hopefully soon. She has been spending her days of late crafting with her amassed "junk," which keeps her occupied and happy for extended periods of time. The staff members here have even been asking for creations from her, so she will be busy for some time. Right now, though, she has put those projects on hold, for she decided she wanted to create something very special for a sweet boy here who hasn't been doing very well the last couple of days. His room is the only one she can see from hers, and normally he is full of crazy antics and joviality, so it concerned her greatly to see him confined to his bed since Friday. Her hope is that her gift will give him reason to smile a bit. I hope and pray, for both their sakes, that she's right.

Today it's been six months since Cassidy was admitted

pre-transplant. It's mind-boggling when I think of it. Our family has been impacted in so many ways outside of what I thought it would be. We have seen and experienced so much—we've had incredible sorrows, but also unimaginable joys. I never dreamed that our life would have been affected in the ways it has. Prior to transplant, we were focused solely on Cassidy's condition and the effect all this upheaval would have on my job, Dave's job, Kali's and Cassidy's school years, our life as a family. Little did we know that all that would be only part of this whole experience (and it's not over yet). It's all very humbling, awe-inspiring, and eye-opening.

June 15: Today, though not a bad day, was not fabulous. Cassidy woke up tired and then proceeded to sleep until 11 a.m. We were then told that she had graduated to eating

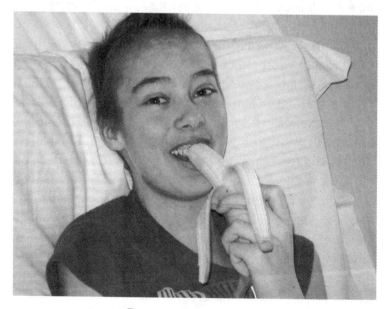

Bananas for a banana!

half a banana and a small dish of applesauce! Cassidy was so very excited! When she received her banana at lunchtime she could hardly contain herself and nibbled at it with a grin from ear to ear.

Then she got sick and it was all for naught.

The rest of the afternoon was spent fighting nausea as best she could without resorting to Gravol (which makes her sleepy). She did some crafting but did not continue on her project for her neighbour.

June 16: We saw the most amazing storm through our windows today! The clouds were black and ominous, and the lightning bolts seemed to travel for miles! Then the rain poured, forming rivers throughout the parking lot below. It was an awe-inspiring event. How great and mighty is the power of our God!

Which is important to remember when dealing with our life. So many little things can, and often do, go wrong. As a mom I just want to take it all away, make everything better, grab my kids and never let go. But then I'm reminded that I'm not the one in control, and I am humbled into realizing that all happens in God's time and in the way he wills it. And I must let go and allow he who is all-powerful to do what he does best.

Cassidy is still struggling with the food. Her first "meal" today came up again, and the nausea stuck around for a good while afterwards. She finally gave in and took some Gravol, and the requisite nap followed. She did find the energy today to finish the hobby horse she's been building for her friend across the hall, though, and he seemed pretty happy to receive it. He's still not doing well, though, so please pray for our friend Travis.

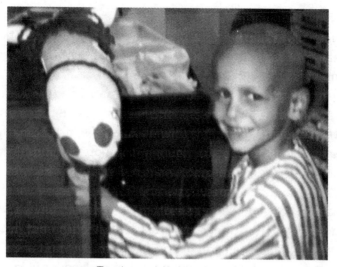

Travis and hobby horse

Please pray for our friend Mike, too. His cancer hasn't responded as well to the chemo as had been hoped, so he will be receiving much stronger chemotherapy over a much longer period of time. Please pray for him and his family as they continue on this often terrifying journey.

So, as the storms rage around us, our lives tossed about, I must turn to the One who has the power to say, "Peace, be still." Shalom.

June 17: Today Cassidy was allowed to eat mashed potatoes. Oooh, I bet you're getting excited, hey? Calm yourselves. The hospital kitchen does not and will not make mashed potatoes without dairy additions. So we couldn't get any sent up for her. The next best thing is a baked potato. But guess what? Yup. Not available either. Thankfully a dear friend of mine stopped in today, and she and I went to Wendy's and picked up a plain-Jane potato for Cass. And a lunch for me :)

Upon our return, Cassidy was grinning from eye to eye (we are talking potatoes here). However, a potato with little seasoning or margarine is…just a potato. She did eat and enjoy some of it, but it lost its appeal quickly. Oh well. What she ate today stayed down, and for that we are both grateful.

June 18: The weather here was a mixed bag of sunshine and thunderstorms. A perfect metaphor for our day.

Cassidy woke at 4 a.m., nauseated. After being sick, she took Gravol and went back to sleep until about 9. She then had some broth (I'm to call it "soup"), and so started her day. The nutritionist came in and informed her she could now have hospital-prepared mashed potatoes (which include dairy products), so she was plenty excited about that. All sunshine.

And then the clouds rolled in. Her doctor came in and told us that there have been some anomalies with some of her blood tests of late (which wasn't news to us), but instead of improving, they have been slowly getting worse. And they don't know why. So it was decided to eliminate many of her meds and her IV food, because they could potentially be causing the problem. She was also scheduled for an ultrasound this afternoon. So besides being off her IV food, she had to go without food altogether until post-ultrasound, which would have been fine, but she didn't get in until after 5 p.m. The girl was hungry!!! She did manage to walk herself all the way to and from radiology unassisted, which was huge, considering she hasn't been out and about at all for a very long time. Also, more blood was taken for further testing. The mother's floodgates were opened—I just want my girl to get better and go home! Sure didn't need any more turbulence…

She did manage to eat a decent serving of the mashed potatoes tonight, and her attitude is positive. She's a lot stronger than her mother, that's for sure.

So please pray. That the blood levels spontaneously normalize. That we receive no more bad news. That she can just continue healing, uninterrupted. That soon she will be able to resume the life of a carefree teen.

I can't wait for clear skies...Peace.

June 20 [because of continued, unexplained high liver enzymes, a liver biopsy was performed to best ascertain the cause of Cassidy's liver anomalies]: Cassidy was rolled into the O.R. at 9 a.m., as scheduled. She was wheeled back about an hour later, after an apparently successful surgery. The results of the biopsy won't be known for a few days yet, but thankfully the doctors are being judicious in getting answers as soon as they can.

Cassidy's on morphine and Gravol around-the-clock, as she got sick this afternoon and the pain was unmanageable. Hopefully this won't carry on too long, for the girl is not eating, not drinking, has no IV nutrition, but more than that, watching her fighting the pain (and she does fight!) is heart-wrenching!

June 21: Cassidy had a good night, free from pain, and mostly restful, which means her mom experienced the same. I laid my worries on the Lord and slept well.

The doctor came in this morning and informed us that *preliminary* results of the biopsy show that whatever is going on in Cassidy's liver is not GVHD! Hallelujah! What a relief! Further tests of the samples will have to be conducted to show the actual cause of her liver enzyme abnormalities, but the initial news is promising.

Thank the Lord for this good news, and take time today to ponder his Good News for all of us. His peace and grace are there for all of us and offer immeasurable comfort. *"But those who hope in the LORD will renew their strength. They will soar on wings like eagles; they will run and not grow weary, they will walk and not be faint"* (Isaiah 40:31, NIV).

June 22: The night is relatively young but promises to be a long one.

This morning started with Cassidy eating some "soup" and crackers. She was then told she'd graduated to a different menu and was presented with some new options. As she was just getting excited about this news, the docs came in and informed her that, because her haemoglobin level had once again dropped—and rather significantly—they wanted an ultrasound of the liver to make sure there was no internal bleeding from the biopsy. So, once again, she had to fast! Dangling a carrot...

Thankfully the ultrasound was done early, and she could resume eating. The ultrasound revealed that there was some internal bleeding due to the biopsy, but it appears to be healing spontaneously. She then had a blood transfusion that went over four hours. No Benadryl this time, however, so that was the good news. The bad news is that, since the transfusion, she's been sick several times and even had a bout of diarrhea. Not good. What caused this is anyone's guess: the transfusion, the change in diet...hopefully nothing more serious than that. She's having a Gravol-induced snooze right now, but Mama's going to be on high alert tonight.

I hate repeating myself every night. I just don't know what else to say or ask of you than "Pray, please."

June 24: Our day today was a real mixed bag. Cassidy summoned up her courage and tried to eat again, and was seemingly successful for a time. Then she was sick again. But she tried again, this time going back to broth, which seemed to agree with her. But then it didn't. So then she waited a while and tried some baked potato chips—which she enjoyed and thought agreed with her. Till it was obvious they hadn't.

So we're experiencing quite the dilemma. She can't go back on IV nutrition because of the possible effects on her already damaged liver (pathology results are still not in), but she can't keep food down long enough to get any value out of it. So we are trying a different drug, which she has been on previously with some success, and hoping that makes a difference. This was decided this evening, so I'm sure the doctors will be discussing at some length tomorrow morning what the best course of action is. Her case is definitely not typical, so a lot of trial and error is at work.

So please pray that very soon her stomach stops treating food as an invader and rather welcomes it as the missed and loved friend it is. Only then can Cassidy move forward toward her long-awaited homecoming.

June 25: I dream of lying on a beach somewhere, white sand under me, sun warming my body, waves gently lapping up on the shore, listening to my girls playing in the water, not a care in the world...

Instead, I lie in a hospital room, watching the world outside continue on, while inside my daughter's life is on hold, waiting.... waiting for her body to accept food...waiting to find out why her nausea and diarrhea continue...waiting for biopsy results...waiting for the next forty-eight hours to pass...waiting for this prescribed dietary fast to be over...waiting for her life to resume...

Cassidy's been put on a fast again to determine if the increased nausea and stool output is due to dietary factors, a possible drug reaction, or the dreadful GVHD. Her day started off okay, with her eating slowly but enjoying the food. An hour later her body once again turned against her, as it had multiple times yesterday. We decided to put her back on the Ondansetron last night, because the Gravol wasn't working, and today we decided to remove the Gravol altogether. It's rare but it is possible that the Gravol is doing the opposite of what it's prescribed to do. Also, because the results of the biopsy are still pending, and her stool volume has increased rather dramatically over the past few days, we decided to start the fast, hoping and praying that as food is removed, her output decreases as well. She was feeling rather miserable for most of the day, but since this decision was made and appropriate measures taken, she's actually been feeling more like herself, much brighter, and almost chipper, although she is completely unimpressed with not being able to eat. Seems like a vicious, never-ending cycle.

But she has not given up hope, and though she is disappointed and upset at the latest developments, she's definitely still fighting and doing whatever she can to get better. So who am I to complain? Tomorrow is another day, and each day holds great opportunity and promise, and every day is a gift from God to be cherished and enjoyed. So I'll pray for new blessings in the morning, and hold on to his promise never to leave us or forsake us.

So I dream of lying on a beach somewhere, white sand under me, sun warming my body, waves gently lapping up on the shore, listening to my girls playing in the water, not a care in the world...

Maybe soon...

June 26: Hang on! We're in for a wild ride!

Last night before bed Cassidy got sick again—vomiting and diarrhea. Her stool volume for the day was way up, as was her mother's fear that something was very wrong. She slept relatively well overnight, until about 6 a.m., when she had a repeat of the evening's event. My heart sunk, and I knew she was in trouble.

Around 10:30 this morning, I was pulled out of the room by a doctor. She took me into a conference room (anxiety-building) and asked me to take a seat. She proceeded to tell me that, since the stool volume had risen so dramatically and had continued to rise after food had been discontinued, there was a high likelihood that the GVHD had returned. There were two options: either wait a few days and see whether it got worse, or start her back on the steroids she'd just been weaned off and try to nip the GVHD in the bud. The risk with waiting is that if you wait too long, it could become out of control, and we'd be right back to square one.

Tough news, to be sure. Restarting the steroids also means delaying Cassidy's eventual homecoming, but I agreed with the docs to be proactive. Whatever we need to do to make my girl well. I figured Cassidy would agree, because I was sure the possibility of the GVHD making a comeback had crossed her mind over the last couple of days. So we went in the room together and broke the news to her. She looked positively shocked and told us very clearly that it wasn't GVHD and she didn't need the steroids. Nonetheless, we decided to move ahead with the treatment. She was also hooked up to the IV nutrition again, as well as a couple of other meds that had been discontinued. The best news she received was that she could eat again! Not that any of the food offered appealed...

Cassidy was pretty disheartened and mainly watched TV for the better part of the day. We had a few visitors, which cheered her up for a spell, and she had some moments of fun, but there was definitely a dark cloud hovering overhead.

Later this afternoon, just after her first dose of the steroids was put in, one of the doctors came in to see how she was doing. To be honest, medically she was doing okay. She had no more "sick" episodes during the day. She told the doctor that she knew intuitively it was not GVHD. He looked at her and laughed (in a kind manner) and told her he hoped she was right. He also said that because the day had gone so well even without the steroids, if things continued to go that way there was no reason why they couldn't stop the steroids as quickly as they had started them. This was definitely good news, but Cassidy was obviously not convinced.

The doctor left the room, closed the door, paused, and re-entered. He turned to the nurse, asked what the stool volume had been for the day, and it had indeed been negligible. He looked at Cassidy and then told her they would stop the steroids now, with the option to restart them any time they felt it was necessary. Cassidy smiled at him and told him again that she knew it wasn't GVHD. He was smiling as he left the room.

I felt a bit like I had motion sickness. Talk about a wild ride! And so nice to have it end on an upswing! Please pray that Cassidy is indeed correct and that it's smooth sailing ahead. Peace.

June 27: The big news for me right now is that Dave is up in Calgary with Cassidy, and I went home with Kali! The plan is that I will be here (God willing) for the week, enjoying my Kali and the summer in my beloved city. It's very strange, and I'm experiencing mixed emotions about it, but it's also exciting. Dave and Cassidy seem to be coping well, and I thank them very much for making this possible for me!

June 28: I hope you all had a restful Sunday with opportunity to spend time with family and friends, enjoy God's creation, and take time to worship him.

That is exactly what I was able to do today and was so blessed by it. I do not know when I'll have the opportunity again, so I just soaked it all up and enjoyed every minute of it! There were times in the day that were tough for me, too, being away from Cassidy, but overall the day was a real blessing for Kali and me, and I thank Dave and my Lord for giving me this time at home.

June 29: I am experiencing very mixed emotions today. Through all the activities of the day, my thoughts weren't far from Cassidy. She didn't have a great day, with more vomiting and increased stool once again. The poor kid keeps trying. It breaks my heart. If only she could just get past this latest, and seemingly endless, hurdle. Please pray...It's been such a long road, and she's been so courageous and strong throughout the journey. I just want her to be able to relax and enjoy the simple pleasures life has to offer.

Tomorrow is another day. Please pray that, wherever my family is, we may enjoy the gifts God has given us, and that the day will shine brightly and be full of promise.

July 2: I met with a good friend this morning for a walk and a coffee, which was physically and spiritually rejuvenating. I guess God knew what I would need to get through the day.

Cassidy did not have an especially good night and woke up early, sick once again. She was supposed to attend a mini-Stampede parade outside with the rest of the kids from her unit but wasn't well enough to. So, disappointed, she watched from the Sunshine Room—a large playroom with many great windows. She was warmed by the sun as she observed the parade. This turned out to be a blessing, as the kids who came in from the outdoors were rather cold! She found that kind of funny and comforting.

The rest of her morning was not a great one. More nausea, diarrhea, and general fatigue. And I think some of the fatigue is due to the lack of progress and repeated disappointments.

Later this afternoon, one of the docs came in and discussed with her and Dave their own uncertainties and frustrations regarding her condition. They really have no evidence-based idea what is going on and why she's not improving. But they're working on it and shared a couple of avenues they're considering. Nothing's been decided, but at least they're working on it...

After that "meeting of the minds," Cassidy's demeanour improved rather substantially. She was still tired, had no appetite, and felt generally unwell, but her spirits lifted considerably. It must have been a huge relief to her to know that something will be done to try to get answers and, hopefully, a resolution. It's been a long road for my sweet girl...

So, the road continues. Where it's going—we don't know. What's coming next—no idea. Why this is happening—we

may never know for sure. When and how it'll be resolved—
the question we'd most like to have answered.

I just trust God will stay beside us the whole way, car-
rying us when necessary. And knowing he is in control of
everything allows me to rest a little easier. Some might find
this a weakness in me, but I'm never stronger than when I
willingly give control of my life over to my Jesus.

July 3: Cassidy had a good day. She was ordered off food,
which also resulted in no sickness. This correlation between
food and nausea/diarrhea has been noted by her docs, and
starting tomorrow she will be following a strict diet of a special formula that should build up the digestive enzymes in
her gut (something that appears to be lacking). Hopefully
this will be the turning point for her—please pray for a
blessing on this food, that it will nourish and heal her in the
way we hope.

July 4: Today was a real mixed bag. I left my home in
Lethbridge, along with Kali, to be reunited with Cassidy and
Dave in Calgary. Once again we were granted traveling mer-
cies, thank God.

Cassidy's day wasn't as positive as she had hoped—it
was decided to keep her off food for another twenty-four
hours, hoping to give the stomach an adequate rest so as not
to skew results once she begins her new diet. Cassidy was
deeply disappointed by this news because she's hungry,
misses the physical aspect of eating, and thought that, had
all gone as planned, she'd be on a relatively normal diet by
now.

But though disappointed, she sure doesn't let it get her
down for long. She is in the process of building a model ship

out of scraps of wood and sticks, and the creative juices are therapeutic medicine. She does not dwell on her problems but finds positive distractions from them. Pretty smart, I'm thinking.

Dave and Kali went home already tonight, as they have important things to attend to tomorrow. So, once again, it's my little girl and me, and though it's hard to leave my home, friends, and family, I'm also blessed to be able to stay here with her.

Please pray that her food tomorrow is blessed and that she will truly be nourished by it.

July 5: Cassidy was supposed to be able to start eating today, but her stool volumes were still too high, so we're hoping for tomorrow. Needless to say, she was rather disappointed, frustrated, and angry over the latest non-development, but she quickly regained her composure. She expertly distracted herself from her hunger with her projects and had (in her words) a "pretty good day." A real testament to her character.

Later this evening, when the halls were quiet and empty, she also initiated a walk. Her doctors have been encouraging this, as she's been sedentary for so long, and tonight she decided to go for it. Regaining her physical strength is something that will have to be accomplished before discharge, and it's something she has some control over, so she set her mind to doing it! I'm a proud mama.

July 6: The day started off with more waiting. Waiting for direction on the whole eating thing, waiting for a decision on whether or not another endoscopy is necessary, waiting...

Early this afternoon Cassidy was given the green light on

the food issue. She is allowed one millilitre every twelve minutes up to a total of five millilitres per hour of Ensure (a nutritional supplement)! Woot, woot! Later on, the gastrointestinal specialists came in and said that they'd wait on doing an endoscopy and/or resuming steroids until they see what happens with Cassidy's digestive system in response to food.

So far, so good.

She got about 17 millilitres in before she started feeling "off." So she slowed down (basically stopped) with the Ensure and got an anti-nausea med on board. And then she lost everything she'd gained.

Very frustrating, discouraging, and disappointing for her. She's tired.

As the day comes to a close, however, I'm noticing more of levity to her mood. She's joking around a bit again, and there are occasional smiles, which, in turn, put a smile on my face.

Tomorrow is a new day, and she's determined to try again. Please continue to pray for a blessing on this treatment. She's getting tired of waiting...

July 8: It's raining again!

Nothing much has changed for Cassidy, either. She's generally weak and tired, yet somehow finds joy in simple things and never gives up trying.

The doctors talked with us at some length today about what we need to do now. It's been decided that tomorrow at some point she will be going into the OR for another scope of her intestines, and they will also be inserting an NG tube down her nasal passage, into the stomach. Very elemental food will then be dripped continuously to the stomach through the NG tube. The scope will hopefully tell them specifically what we are dealing with so that, if more treatment is required, that, too, will commence soon. Though by no means happy with this new development, Cassidy has agreed to go ahead with it all. Brave girl.

May the Son shine upon us all!

July 9: *"Pray without ceasing, give thanks in all circumstances; for this is the will of God in Christ Jesus for you"* (1 Thessalonians 5:17-18).

Today was a day where I truly had to give everything over to God. Cassidy had a scope and biopsies of her lower bowel, and the prep for that is something no mother should ever have to do to her child, and I hope I never will again. Yet, better me than a stranger. And I sincerely pray that Cassidy will never be put through that again.

Preliminary results of the scope show that the GVHD is likely not resolved but somewhat improved. We will have to wait for the biopsy results to have a truer picture of what we are dealing with and how to best treat it. Not great news, but we knew that something was wrong, and now I pray we can move ahead. I thank God for the technology available that make these tests possible.

She also had an NG tube inserted, and I pray that this will indeed be another step to healing. Thankfully there are formulas available that should be able to give her the nutrition possible, and I pray that soon the IV nutrition can be halted.

She had a pretty rough day, but at the end of it she was once again finding things to laugh at, activities to give her pleasure, and ways to end the day on a positive note. I thank God for blessing her with an amazing amount of positivity, and I pray that it's something she never loses. Even the doctor called her a "real trouper"! God's grace evidenced in a young woman.

Now it's a matter of waiting and seeing what the future has in store for us. I pray that real progress will begin soon and that whatever treatments are warranted will be blessed by the Great Physician. I thank God for the doctors who work tirelessly to bring my daughter back to full health.

"Pray without ceasing, give thanks in all circumstances; for this is the will of God in Christ Jesus for you" (1 Thessalonians 5:17-18).

July 10: "Never be afraid to trust an unknown future to a known God."—Corrie ten Boom.[7]

And there are many unknowns. What we do know is this: The biopsies have shown that there definitely is unresolved GVHD still present in Cassidy's gut. This, however, is not necessarily bad news, because the biopsies also showed significant improvement throughout. So, obviously, the GVHD responded to the treatments Cassidy has had over the past months, and that is fabulous news! It also means that the doctors have a ready action plan and have already restarted the steroids and the process to acquire more MSCs. I never thought I'd be thankful to hear "GVHD" as my child's diagnosis, but it really could have been much, much worse.

We do not know how well or quickly Cassidy's body will respond.

We do not know when she'll be able to start eating again.

We do not know how long she'll remain hospitalized.

But we do know our God is good, and he knows. And in him is where we'll put our trust.

July 11: Today it's been 200 days since Cassidy's stem cell transplant! Unreal, but very real all at once. Tomorrow will be three months since readmission. Wow. How our lives have changed!

Dave and Kali are here today, and that always makes for a better day. Cassidy had a good night and the day has been rather mundane—which is always a positive in our world! No sickness, no tests, some crafting, watching of television and movies, and a walk through the unit. The doctors say that tests show the GVHD to be at stage three, but I'll take that over the stage four she was at a couple of months ago! She is much better physically, spiritually, and emotionally than she was then. And knowing something's being done to improve her situation has definitely put a sparkle back in her eyes. And mine.

That's not to say she's out of the woods—by no means! But already today, after just a couple doses of the steroids and the tube feeds, there seems to be some improvement. Only time will tell, but we take everything a day (or minute) at a time here. So for today, I thank God for the little bit of light on what has been a long, often dark, road.

Dave and Kali are doing okay. They definitely have their own individually unique burdens and trials, but, all in all, it looks like they are coping well. Good friends, good co-workers, a good church family, and a good God make all the difference. Thanks once again to all who have offered them support and companionship through what could be (and sometimes is) a very lonely journey. Sunday afternoon they leave again for home, so tonight I'm enjoying the company of one daughter while Dave enjoys the other, and tomorrow we'll trade off again.

July 13: Today was the best day Cassidy's had in the past week. She was able to sleep in (after a less than restful night) and woke up hungry. That was not a positive but is a sign that there is healing in the gut. She, in her own blessedly determined way, found ways to distract herself from the hunger and proceeded to do some foil etching. She also had the energy for a shower and dressing changes—rather tiring tasks. The etching she worked on for the better part of the day, after which she took a walk through the unit and then gave a quick lesson in origami to one of the nurses.

Presently, however, she's once again feeling a bit "off," a feeling that last night precipitated her being sick. We'll pray that doesn't happen again tonight.

The doctors are telling us their plans—which right now I don't pay much heed to. The last time they started giving us timelines, they projected Cassidy's discharge date as July 16. Obviously that is not going to happen, so we'd rather just take everything a day at a time and hope we continue moving forward. For the first time in a long time, while there was a storm raging outside all day, it was not in here! I'm going to have to start using a different analogy!

And I thank my God, who has the power to calm the storms.

July 16: Cassidy continues to improve—thank God! Her nutrient drip is increased every eight hours, and she is now getting 45 millilitres per hour. She is hungry, but managing, and the important thing is that her body seems to be handling the food! Her energy level is still low, but she did manage a thirty-minute stroll—*outside*—today! She's keeping herself busy with metal etching art at this time and doing a fantastic job of it. Doctors and nurses are pleased and (cautiously) optimistic.

July 19: Cassidy was mostly good today—she managed some etching, her shower, dressing changes, and cap changes and still had some energy left to go outside and enjoy some beautiful sunshine! Later this evening, however, she started feeling "off" again, and, as seems to be the pattern, got sick late tonight. They are trying to adjust her feeds to eliminate this annoying and counterproductive reaction, but further tweaking is obviously needed.

July 21: Day 100 since readmission! Wow! To think post-transplant we were home at this point gives me pause.

At the same time, though, Cassidy is so much improved over what she was 100 days ago, and for that I am immensely grateful. Today, however, was not a particularly "up" day, though better than some. She was permitted to eat today but did not feel physically well enough to give it a try. And later on this afternoon, she once again got sick, and she ended up dislodging her NG tube in the process. Definitely not a pleasant experience, and neither was the insertion of a new tube. But she did it without any fuss, thanks to the skilled hands of her nurse. (Thank you!)

July 23: *"Be strong, and let your heart take courage, all you who wait for the LORD!"* (Psalm 31:24).

Well, Cassidy has been blessed with courage, that's for sure. She took her enzymes this morning, intending to "try, try again," but promptly "lost" them. But did she give up? Oh no! A while later she was trying to eat—and managed a whole six grams before she begged off. Not a significant amount by any stretch, but it stayed down all day. Which is saying something—I'm just not sure what.

July 24: The TPN (intravenous nutrition) has been discontinued because Cassidy is now getting adequate nutrition through the NG tube. Please pray this is a permanent change.

The dose of steroids has had a small decrease, something they hope to do slowly but regularly. Please pray that her body reacts well to the change and that the weaning off meds can continue as planned.

Cassidy was given a menu of foods she can choose from—very boring and bland, but it's a start. Pray that she is able to tolerate everything she ingests.

She had a moment today when she once again got sick and once again lost her NG tube in the process, so that was not pleasant. However, that was really the only negative in a dull but positive day. Dave got off work a bit early so was able to join us late afternoon, and we all went for a stroll outside. Kali was kindly driven by a cousin down to Calgary from the camping trip she was on, so we are all back together in Calgary.

So, though we're not where we want to be and things aren't progressing as speedily as we'd like, there is still a lot to be grateful for.

Please thank God for every good thing. And pray that there is much more good to come.

July 25: We all went outside for a half hour this afternoon and played cards in the shade. Amazing what we used to take for granted! This is truly precious time for us, and especially for Cassidy, as she is able to be unhooked from all the tubes and meds for a short time every day. She had another episode of vomiting and again lost her NG tube, but reinserting it is becoming not as big a deal. Hopefully, however, this won't become part of the norm for her.

July 27: Today was a hard day for many reasons. Cassidy felt poorly for most of the day but did perk up late afternoon. We decided to hold her feeds for a while, and that seemed to help her out, but we don't yet know the significance of that.

As many of you already know through an email I sent earlier, friends of ours whose dear son died here in January lost their home in a fire Saturday. This breaks my heart. I can't imagine what they are going through at this time, and I can't take away their hurt and pain. So I'll pray God will make his presence felt in their lives, and I'll be here for them if they need me.

It came to my attention today as well that a friend of the family is also facing cancer. Once again there is so little I can do but ask he who is Comfort to be with the family and provide them their every need. And offer my friendship. You are loved!

But then I heard that a young woman who was here for a brain tumour was given a clean bill of health and allowed to go home. This I smile about and thank my Lord for. I also spent time talking to my family tonight, as I always do, but today especially counted it as a blessing. I also spent time talking with a dear friend, who patiently helped me deal with some issues. Also a blessing.

By the close of Cassidy's day, she was feeling better and stronger. She took care of a few personal chores and even managed a walk through the unit.

And there's hope that tomorrow will be even better.

August 1: Cassidy woke up this morning in good spirits, which lasted through the bulk of the day. Later in the day, after Cassidy's third feed, however, she once again started feeling "icky," and the feeling didn't go away until a third of the way through her fourth feed. She lost a lot of what she's gained over the past few hours but only minutes later continued the feed (her determination is inspiring!) and completed it without further incident. She felt fine again afterwards. More tweaking may be warranted, I'm thinking.

August 3: To all who sent my sweet Cassidy cards, gifts, letters, emails, and notes of congratulations on her fifteenth birthday, may I say "Thank you!"

Today was a stellar day. Cassidy awoke to her nurse writing birthday greetings on her window, and then most of the nurses came into the room to sing "Happy Birthday" to her. Shortly thereafter Dave and Kali arrived, and we had a family birthday celebration.

She opened gifts (not just from us) and cards, all the while with a beautiful smile upon her beautiful face. Then a good family friend and his two young daughters showed up—bearing more gifts and a box full (!) of cards from our church family. Wonderful! She took her time reading through them, and we all visited for a spell.

Then it was time for Kali and me to ready a special room for the surprise of the day. We spent some time decorating, and then we ushered in the special guests. You see, the mother of one of Cassidy's friends offered to plan a party for her and drove up from Lethbridge with four of Cassidy's friends. They brought games, crafts, cake, and other fun stuff, and all we had to do was provide a time and a place! Fabulous!

We had it all arranged with the doctors and nurses, who were almost as excited as we were. Cassidy, however, though she knew something was afoot, didn't have a clue as to what was really going on! The doctors agreed to ease off on the feeds for the day, so she wouldn't be at all uncomfortable, and the nurses were great about making the timing of the meds work with the timing of the surprise.

Leah, Jenna, Cassidy, Taylor, Jessica and Kali

So, when the time was right, Dave and I ushered her to the room, we opened the door, and *"Surprise!!!!"* And she was surprised! There were tears, and not just from her, but mostly there was joy, which lasted to the very end of the day. The girls played games, did a craft, and were just typical teenage girls—so good for Cassidy! The party lasted about three hours. Thanks to *all* who made it possible.

After the guests left, Dave and Kali too had to go. And then it was just the two of us again. Cassidy gave me a big hug, said "thank you," and told me that, despite the circumstances, this was the "best birthday ever"! I have to agree.

Thank God for all good things. Give praise to him!

August 4: This morning we were wakened early because Cassidy had to go for her 100-day post-MSC-infusion CT scan. So after ingesting some contrast fluid, she walked herself to diagnostic imaging and went through the paces.

Early this afternoon, we had the results. The GVHD in the gut appears to be resolved! Praise God for this news! There is something else going on in the gut, however, that causes some concern, but not enough at this point for the doctors to change their plans regarding her care. So we're continuing with further tweaking of her feeds (I think we're on the right track now) and just more wait-and-see. Other than that, today was a blessed one, with Cassidy happily crafting, and she even got up to do some organizing of all her accumulated treasures!

August 5: Cassidy had a good day! Because of the adjustments to her feeds, her energy level is up and her demeanour overall is a lot more chipper and spirited. It's still quite the process to work through to get her to where she'll be able to eat normally, but any improvement is reason to give thanks.

Cassidy and I read a devotional tonight based on the verse *"But it came to pass..."* from Judges 15:1 (KJV). The story was told about a woman who faced many hardships in her life but continued to come back to the comfort of this verse. In her words, "We have God!...And we know he will take care of us. We can look at the misery around us and know that God will see us through. Then we can smile and say, 'It came to pass.'"[8]

And Cassidy's been through a lot and continues to have problems and issues with her health. But we can look back on at least some of it and say "It came to pass."

Please pray for the day when we can say the same of it all!

August 7: Two great events occurred today: Dave and Kali came for the weekend. And Cassidy was switched from a continuous infusion of her immunosuppressant to an oral dose. Which means she will now be granted passes (!!!!) for a couple of hours every day, as she wants or needs them! This is fantastic news! Tomorrow we hope to go out and about as a whole family for a while—something that hasn't happened since April. Please pray that our time is blessed, that she continues to improve, and that this really is the next step to complete recovery.

August 8: Our weekend was a good one. As you know, Cassidy was able to leave the hospital for a couple of hours. Per her request, we all took a ride in the car. We toured downtown Calgary and 17th Avenue, just looking at all the people out on a nice summer's day. And there were a lot of "colourful" people! Kali sat in the back with Cassidy and provided a running commentary, which is always amusing. Cassidy had a smile on her face the entire time!

August 10: Today was a very exciting day for Cassidy and all of us involved in her life. She was given the option of eating almost anything she wanted (within certain guidelines, of course), and so she enjoyed some fresh veggies and a couple of warm chocolate chip cookies!!! And, so far, there have been zero negative effects! Praise God! This evening we went for a walk outside, and I worked her hard—going up and down hills at a good pace. She was hurting and tired, but she kept smiling—shows her determination and spirit once again.

There's also talk of a sooner-than-expected discharge from the hospital. Whether this comes to pass depends on a number of factors, but we may be moving back into the RMH shortly. It will still be some time before we can go home, but we've learned to take things one day at a time and trust God to work out the details.

I think that's all I have for you—but I think it's plenty!
Thank God for all good things—praise be to Him!

August 11:

2 1/4 fish sticks
1 chocolate chip cookie
1/2 Italian sub sandwich
1 yogurt
4 baby carrots with ranch dip
water

Gives a whole meaning to being thankful for, and asking a blessing upon, your food!

August 12: Well, it's been four months today since Cassidy's readmission to hospital, but the end may very well be in sight! She ate full meals today without any negative effects, so I humbly and sincerely thank God for his gracious care of my sweet daughter! Tomorrow or Friday the doctors are hoping to remove the one central line from her arm (surgery), which is huge! But also requires prayer. Then the plan is, for Friday, to *move out of here into the Ronald McDonald House*!!!!! We have no idea how long we will have to stay there, but it is one more step towards going home. And for that I can only say, "Thank you, Lord!"

August 13: Well, another big day, though a long one. We spent the entire day waiting for an O.R. to be available, which also meant Cassidy couldn't eat that entire time. Very frustrating—because she's very hungry!!! Finally at 4:10, she was taken up to the O.R., the PICC line was removed without incident, and she was back in her room eating before 5:30!! And eat, she did! Very fabulous! And now I have to pack, because sometime this weekend it looks like we're out of here!!!!!!!!

August 14: We have moved some of our belongings into RMH; Cassidy is on an "overnight pass," just until all our belongings are packed and relocated. Then she will be officially discharged!

August 15: Today was a busy, but good, day. Cassidy had to be at the hospital at nine o'clock for blood work, and we got the remainder of the packing done. Then we did some grocery shopping, the girls watched some TV and helped unpack, I did some laundry, and then I (!!!!!!) cooked! And it actually tasted good! Not bad for someone as rusty as me!

It was a busy day, though, and Cassidy's had more exercise the last two days than she has in the last four months altogether! So she's a bit tuckered, and everyone (but me) went to bed early tonight. Tomorrow Dave's folks, his sis and bro-in-law, and two kidlets come for a visit before heading to Lethbridge for the most of the week. So should be another busy, but good, day!

I hope you all have a blessed Sunday. Take time for what it was intended!

August 17: This morning had Cassidy and me walking to the hospital for a 9:00 appointment. She did well, but by the time we made it back to the house three hours later (it takes time to see a doctor, apparently!), she was pretty tired and stiff. Amazing how four months in bed can do that to a body! All went well at the hospital, and she was formally discharged as planned. Which is good, because our room there no longer looks at all cozy!

The rest of the day went well, with Cassidy spending the better part of it with Leigha, the recreation coordinator here. Good for her to get away from her mama for a while! Then this evening there was a campfire and wiener roast outside, and that was a lot of fun! Actually gave us (her) a real taste of what summer should be!

Cassidy and Leigha

August 22: Today was a full but good day. We spent time driving around the city again (Cassidy loves this, and it doesn't tire her), bought groceries, rented movies, and this afternoon and evening were spent watching said videos. Pretty mundane, but around these parts mundane is good!

One thing causing a bit of concern today is the level of immunosuppressant in Cassidy's blood. The level on Friday was much higher than that taken on Tuesday, with no under-stood cause. This means further tweaking of her meds, and an appointment at clinic on Monday for another test. Please pray it's just a blip that ends up meaning nothing. Other than that, all is well.

August 25: We had clinic again yesterday, and further tweaking of meds is necessary once again. Nothing overly concerning but something we need to take seriously and get on top of. Physically, however, Cassidy is still doing well, and she was happy to say "No" to the doctor's questions about possible symptoms! Very happy—almost sassy!

In the afternoon she attended a day camp put on here at the RMH by the YMCA. So that kept her busy for a good four hours, after which we jumped into a van and made our way to the southeast end of the city to take in the Global Fest Fireworks competition. RMH had a private tent away from the crowds, making it possible for Cassidy or other immunosuppressed children to attend. We had a great time, and it was definitely good for her to be out and about—though a little hard on her mother's nerves! Stepping out of the comfort zone!

August 27: Another good day, with nothing new to report. Cassidy is still doing reasonably well and is determined to regain her strength. That girl has more determination in her little finger than I do in my entire being!

Tomorrow we have clinic again, and further tweaking of med doses will likely be in order. Please pray that they can find a balance soon. Dave and Kali will be arriving once again, and Saturday Kali and I will be heading home to Lethbridge. I haven't missed her first day of school yet, and the softy in me doesn't want to miss this one (her last, by the way) either! So Dave will hold down the fort here while I am home for about a week.

September 7: The week went well for all of us. Dave and Cassidy stayed here in Calgary, and thanks to some female assistance, they remained well-fed and clothed! Really, they had a good time together, Dave was able to catch some extra sleep, and I think the break was good for both of them.

I spent a couple of days with Kali before school started—shopping, running errands, and just hanging out. Then Wednesday I dropped her off at school and later attended her opening assembly. Was good to see students and colleagues again, but strange at the same time.

The rest of my weekdays were spent doing things I wanted to do—some shopping, some time with precious people, and some relaxing and enjoying "me" time. And my evenings with Kali—what could be sweeter?

She and I returned to Calgary on Saturday, and we spent the time till Sunday afternoon as a whole family. Today Dave and Kali are enjoying a day of R and R (deserved), including time at the church picnic. Cassidy's crafting (surprise!), and I'm on the computer (surprise!). Tomorrow she has clinic again, and I'll fill you in on the medical side of her life.

September 8: This morning started off with a two-hour visit to clinic, the results of which determined that Cassidy will be seen in clinic again tomorrow. Her liver enzymes continue to be elevated, as do her immunosuppressant levels. What this means is unclear, but she may be undergoing further testing this week, including an ultrasound. Please pray that a resolution to these issues is timely and simple.

Other than that, the day was relatively positive, but quiet. I hope to start Cassidy on school work this week, so I'm savouring the peace and tranquility now. Could be very interesting!!!!

September 10: Need to start tonight by wishing and praying for my daughter Kali to have a

Happy, Happy 17th Birthday!!!!!!!!!!!!!!!!!!!!!!!!

She's an incredible girl who has become an incredible young woman and has handled this past year with grace, humour, maturity, and faith. I am so very proud to be her mother, and I truly hope her day, and the coming year, are blessed. Love you, Kali!!!

Cassidy and I were in clinic at 9:15 this morning, to meet with GI docs. We didn't end up seeing them till 11, however, so there went our morning! Then at 12 she was called in for an ultrasound of her liver. Preliminary results show nothing untoward happening there, so for that we are greatly relieved and thankful. We have another meeting with GI in the morning, so please pray that goes well and there are no more surprises at hand. It appears that her elevated immunosuppressant levels were due to a simple error in taking her blood from the wrong lumen, but this will also be confirmed tomorrow or Friday through further tests. Whether this is tied in with the elevated liver enzymes has yet to be determined. But so far things are looking up. Please pray this to continue.

Other than that (!), the day was uneventful, and we sincerely hope for that to be the case throughout the week. Exciting is not what we want! Although I am thankful for all the good in our lives. We have been blessed through trying circumstances, and that is humbling and faith-building.

September 11: Cassidy's liver enzymes are still rising. We've raised her steroid and immunosuppressant dosages, and now just hope and pray that the changes make a difference to her liver. Tuesday she'll be tested again, and at that time it will be decided whether they will go ahead with the biopsy they have scheduled for her.

September 13: Just a quick email tonight to ask you to continue to pray for Cassidy. A few more little issues have come up, so the next few days may be very important to her, and to us (her family). Please pray that if there are problems, they can be treated easily and quickly. It's been nine months as of today since she was admitted to hospital pre-transplant, and all we really want to do at this point is have our "normal" lives back. We hope and pray for that to happen soon.

September 14: We had clinic today and saw a doctor who took a look at some of the things that have been causing Cassidy grief as of late. It was determined that she is likely suffering from a thrush infection, so she's been started on a med for that. Hopefully it works quickly and effectively and creates no further problems for her. This could also be contributing to her lessened appetite.

Tuesday we go to clinic again, and liver enzyme levels will be drawn. Unless there is a substantially positive change in the numbers, Cassidy is scheduled for a liver biopsy on Wednesday. So please: Pray on! I see the benefit in a biopsy, because it gives us clear answers and allows treatment to begin in a timely fashion. The procedure still gives me angst, however, as it does Cassidy. She's dreading it mostly because the last one they performed gave her pain. Circumstances are dramatically different this time, though, so I hope and pray the experience will be as well.

September 15: Today was another rollercoaster day. Cassidy had clinic at 9 a.m., where they drew blood for a multitude of tests (including pre-surgery ones), and she saw a doctor for a physical exam. Her thrush is marginally better but still bothers her a fair bit when she eats—not what my beyond-slim girl needs! We then discussed with the doctor the plans for the surgery. The biggest issue that came to light today was the fact that now that Cassidy's back on high-dose steroids and her immunosuppressant level is being opti-mized, her liver enzymes are actually going down! This is good news, but also rather accurately identifies the problem in the liver as GVHD. Not good news, but at least this time the standard treatment for it seems to be working.

Then later today the doc discussed with the folks from GI what to do about surgery. I had two thought processes at play: first, any time you can avoid surgery, you should; and second, I just want to know conclusively what is going on so it can be treated early and well. The problem for me in can-celling the surgery is the question of waiting too long, and then if things go terribly wrong we're behind the eight ball. But, thankfully, it wasn't my decision to make. I simply prayed to God that the right conclusion would be made.

Later this afternoon, the hospital called, informing me that the surgery had been cancelled. Cassidy's relief was pal-pable! She will be going to clinic again on Thursday to have the tests repeated, but for now she's just enjoying the news.

So how does her mother feel? Grateful, yet anxious. Happy, yet cautious. Make sense? Not to me, either, but it is what it is.

So please pray that the drugs keep doing their job, and that the GVHD is successfully treated, and that further surgeries will be unwarranted.

The rest of the day was good, and Cassidy is much happier and more relaxed than she has been for days. Thank God for this.

September 17: Good news from the clinic today! Cassidy's liver enzymes are almost in the normal range, and her immunosuppressant is finally at a therapeutic level! Praise God! She'll be going to the hospital on Saturday for a recheck, and possibly some further tweaking of meds, but as of right now, things are definitely looking a lot brighter!

A thoughtful and generous friend also told us today that she's going to lend us a vehicle for the duration of our stay, so that will afford Cassidy and me a bit more freedom. Thanks, JB!

September 22: Clinic today. All her blood levels were okay, though the liver enzymes aren't quite where they'd like them to be yet. Further tweaking of meds!

We went for a walk to a pond and fed the ducks there. Later this afternoon we went for another drive and ended up in the country! Was a real treat to be able to see the beautiful fall colours outside of the city—especially with the sun shining brightly and the windows open! What a beautiful day!

Tomorrow Cassidy officially starts school. I hope the setup here and the materials she'll be using will be good for her. Tenth grade is important, and for many reasons it's important she does well.

September 29: Today was another good day, with a good checkup and mostly positive news on test results. Cassidy did not have school today but did some reading from her Social text. Good times! We had a visit from a friend from Lethbridge, so that broke up the afternoon a bit. Supper was prepared for us, so that negated my having to cook supper, and that is also always welcome.

So, overall, today went well. Tomorrow Cassidy will have school in the morning, and then hopefully we'll get out for a spell. I hear rumours of snow coming soon, so we might as well enjoy the few fall days we are blessed with.

I know my updates of late have not been exciting or all too interesting, but for that I am thankful—it means life for us is on an even keel, and after the tumultuous waters we've traversed, some smooth-sailing is most welcome!

Thanks for your prayers. Thanks for your support. Thanks for caring.

September 30: Another good day. School, lunch, a drive to the downtown (yup, I'm getting brave!), a potluck dinner, and time to chill. Really, what more could one ask for? Okay, plenty. But I'll keep counting my blessings and being grateful for all that is good. I hope you all are able to do the same.

And I'll keep praying for more of the good.

October 2: Thursday Cassidy had school all morning and worked most of the afternoon on her assignments. We also spent some time with our pastor, who came to visit us. We miss our church family and attending services, so this visit was most welcome. In the evening Cassidy and I went for a walk outside. Looks (and feels) like winter is going to hit us here this weekend, so we figured we'd enjoy the mild weather once more.

Today Cassidy had clinic, and blood work shows that her liver enzymes continue to drop, and her weight continues to rise! Great news on both fronts! This afternoon Cassidy did more school work for a while, and then we went for another drive through the city's core.

Dave and Kali arrived this evening. We had a pleasant supper together, played a Canadian trivia game, and then watched a movie. Tomorrow calls for snow, so it will be interesting to see what the day holds for us.

October 6: All went reasonably well at clinic today. Blood counts were mostly good, although the liver enzymes are starting to creep up a bit again. So, further tweaking of meds! But Cassidy's weight is also up—to over eighty-five pounds—so that is great news!

The best news, though, is that the doctors granted Cassidy permission (barring any illness in the family or herself) to go home for the Thanksgiving weekend! She will not be able to participate in traditional family or church gatherings, but she is very excited just at the prospect of being in her own room, in her own house, in her own city, with her own dog...

So, friends, we've a lot to be thankful for this Thanksgiving. And all praise must be given to God, who has brought us safely this far.

October 13: Cassidy and I had a great weekend at home. It was good for Dave and Kali, too, especially since they didn't need to come to Calgary in order to see us. Cassidy was most excited to see her friends outside after school Friday and also to hold her dog, Mikey, for the first time in six months! The weekend was mostly relaxing, and for me the highlight was being able to attend church, all three services, over the weekend! Definitely a blessing! Sunday we had a non-traditional Thanksgiving meal with my mom. Thanksgiving Day started with church and then a simple meal at home before Cassidy and I left again for Calgary.

We arrived at the Ronald McDonald House late afternoon, just in time for a traditional turkey dinner, which had been prepared by a local software company. Great of them to give up their time on their holiday to serve those families here at the house!

Today was clinic again, and some numbers are up, and some are down. Nothing alarming—really just more of the same. Further tweaking of meds!!! Cassidy has really started to regain some of her weight and is now just shy of eighty-eight pounds! Good news! She baked chocolate chip cookies tonight and kept quite a stash for herself—weight gain should continue!

That's about it from snowy, winter-like Calgary. Hopefully the weather improves a bit yet this week. We don't seem to have had much of a fall!

Thanks for the notes of encouragement and support, the cards and letters we receive, the monetary support, but mostly, thanks for the prayers said on our behalf. This was truly a Thanksgiving weekend!

October 15: Nothing much to report so far this week. Cassidy has been having "school" this week and has been pretty busy with that. We also have been a bit housebound, as snow hit Calgary this week with a vengeance! Today saw it melting, though. Hopefully that'll be it for snowfall until winter officially begins. I know, wishful thinking! But a girl's allowed to wish...

If the weather remains mild, and if clinic goes well again tomorrow, doctors say that we can once again go home for the weekend! So pray this is the case, and also that it can be a regular occurrence. It would be good for all concerned...A little taste of normality...Don't quite remember what that is!

October 16: Cassidy and I are once again in Lethbridge for the weekend! We left clinic this morning and went into the prepacked car and headed for the open road. Cassidy again was able to see her friends as they left school for the day, and I, too, met up with a few of mine.

Her tests came out about the same as usual, and she's just shy of ninety pounds now and very much enjoying her food!

October 20: Cassidy and I returned to Calgary after a nice break at home. The weekend went quickly, but we were able to spend some good time together as a family, and it makes it a bit easier to come back up here to Calgary. Physically, Cassidy is doing well. Her weight continues to rise, and her overall appearance and demeanour is one of health. Medically, however, it's still basically a process of managing her symptoms. Whenever we tweak her meds, her liver enzymes rise, which likely means that the GVHD is still present there. Thankfully, though, she has no other symptoms, and it looks like it's just a matter of time and patience.

So please keep praying for a complete and permanent recovery, and, as the flu season and the H1N1 virus appear to be significant threats, pray for protection from those viruses—for her, but also for our whole family.

October 27: We spent a good weekend at home, returning to Calgary Monday afternoon. We had a nice dinner and then played the compulsory bingo game in the evening. This morning Cassidy had clinic. Her physical exam showed no significant changes, as did her blood tests. We are going to attempt another wean off steroids, so please pray that her liver enzymes remain stable, so that the wean can continue. Getting her off the steroids is the main hurdle right now that needs to be passed before we can go home for good.

Tomorrow she and I are going to go for our H1N1 vaccination. This virus has us a little nervous, but we will again trust that God will provide us whatever we need (including the vaccination!). Please pray that there are no complications and that we, as well as all those we love and care for, are protected from what could well be a pandemic. Pray, too, that no other viruses or infections threaten Cassidy's fragile health.

November 4: Well, we're back in Calgary, at least until Friday. Cassidy's tests Tuesday showed favourable results, so the weaning off prednisone continues! She still has intermittent health issues, and these are being followed carefully, but she continues to gain weight and seems to be regaining her strength. The biggest news is that her central line (Broviac) is scheduled to be removed next Thursday! This is great news—it means no more dressing changes, cap changes, heparin locks...less bother. It also means that, after eleven months with the Broviac, her skin will finally be able to breathe and heal from all that time with dressings. Cassidy is very excited! It will be a relatively simple day surgery, so hopefully we'll still make it home on Friday for the weekend.

November 9: Cassidy and I returned to Calgary this afternoon after another weekend home. The weekend consisted mainly of family time, plus I was blessed by two church services on

Sunday. I needed the reminders of God's grace and mercy for his children—no matter who they are, where they live, or what they've done in their lives. It was also good to be surrounded by people who genuinely care for each other, who only wish God's best for one another, who lift each other up, and who share in each other's joys and sorrows.

Tomorrow Cassidy goes in to have her Broviac removed. Though a simple procedure, your prayers for her safety are coveted. She has clinic first in the morning, and the surgery is scheduled for early afternoon. I will inform you when she comes out of recovery. Other than that, the week looks like more of the same, and hopefully a return trip to Lethbridge on the weekend.

November 22: Cassidy is now Broviac- and dressing-free and is most excited about this fact! She is now able to shower normally and needs not be as careful physically. She is feeling well over-all and, besides the regular ups and downs, is doing well medically. As you know, she and I have been coming home regularly for the weekends. This past week she spent with Dave in Calgary, and I stayed home with Kali. It was a good week for all of us, and necessary for me as the prospects for returning home permanently look more promising. When, you might ask? Nothing's certain, but it could be relatively soon. I will have to have a long and intense discussion with the doctors this week and see what comes of that.

But for now, we're enjoying every day, especially the days at home. Tomorrow Dave heads back to work, Kali to school, and Cassidy and I back up to Calgary. Please pray all goes well for all of us and that we'll all be home together again soon.

November 26: Well, it's happened! After 347 days (give or take some weekends) in Calgary, Cassidy and I have returned home! Today was a crazy day, with packing and cleaning of our room at the Ronald McDonald House, but we got it done and were home early in the afternoon. There are going to be a lot of adjustments to be made and added stresses now that we've left our "safety net," so please pray that the transition goes well and that, indeed, we are home to stay!

Cassidy will be having weekly blood tests here in Lethbridge, but if all continues to go well, our clinic visits in Calgary will only be once every two weeks. Her schooling will continue, but at home with yours truly as her support, so prayer is needed for that endeavour as well—I don't want her to grow to resent me!

Great friends!

Tomorrow a couple of her friends are coming over for a few hours—much needed social interaction with much missed girls! Hopefully this visit is the beginning of many. She's still unable (medically) to go where there are large groups of people, so getting appropriate social interaction is a challenge. But one I'm determined to meet!

Please pray that she is on the road to a complete recovery, our stay here in Lethbridge will be permanent, and soon our life in Calgary will be nothing but a memory. Thank God for the progress thus far! I thank you all from the bottom of my heart for all the support you've offered over the past year...I really don't know where we'd be if it wasn't for the kindness of friends and strangers.

PART THREE

Almost a year post-transplant, we returned home. Christmas decorations were being hung as we packed to leave the Ronald McDonald House, and we were so grateful not to have to stay for a second Christmas. We had experienced every holiday of the year either in hospital or at the house.

Finally at home, Cassidy began a routine of doing school-work by correspondence and getting together periodically with friends. Life started becoming normal, a new normal, including regular checkups in Calgary and ongoing changes to medication doses as new challenges were faced and dealt with. The future is still very uncertain—with still some evidence of GVHD present—but we are grateful for all we've been blessed with, and we count each new day a gift.

Unfortunately, on June 6 of 2010 Cassidy ended up in the Alberta Children's Hospital. Once again I will let my updates relay the details.

June 6: Another update, six months since the last...

I hope you all had opportunity to worship our God this weekend, something I value more and more.

I did attend church this morning, and then rushed home to pack for a stay in Calgary. Earlier this week, Cassidy was feeling rather fatigued, but otherwise well. She then developed cold symptoms and subsequently what seemed to be a bit of asthma (not uncommon for her when fighting a cold). Worrisome, to be sure, but not desperately so.

Friday night, however, things seemed to take a turn for the worse, and when on Saturday morning she was also complaining of an earache, I knew a visit to the local ER was in order. So off we went.

Several tests, x-rays, the advice of two brilliant doctors, and more than a few tears later, Cassidy and Dave were in an ambulance on their way to the Alberta Children's Hospital. It appears she is suffering from pneumonia and needs extra oxygen to keep her levels at an acceptable level. She is also being aggressively treated with antibiotics, so hopefully this is a simple pneumonia, and she can return home soon.

Kali and I stayed in Lethbridge that night to tie up loose ends, but after the Sunday morning worship service, and some last minute packing and lunch, Kali and I were on our way up to Calgary. She and Dave left to return home to work and school soon thereafter. It's very strange to be back here. We are in a familiar room that belonged to friends of ours previously (Nick and Maddie most recently) and directly across from the executive suite we inhabited for all those months.

So here I am. Sitting on my bed, back resting against the north wall, laptop on my, well, lap...window to my left...with a view of the cafeteria to the east and a park and river valley to the south...We can see, through the door's window, the view from our old room as well. All rooms but Cassidy's and one other on this wing are vacant.

Cassidy is doing okay. She really needs the oxygen—if she goes to the bathroom without, on her return she's gasping, and the oxygen levels drop rapidly—but she's upright and crafting and enjoying her remote control once again. Hopefully the antibiotics are effective, and, pending results of other tests, the docs are hoping to send her home on oral antibiotics in a few days. Would be nice, but...we'll see. I'm a little numb, and a bit afraid of being too optimistic. But God knows, and that's what matters. His grace is sufficient.

Please pray that Cassidy recovers quickly and completely, and also that Kali is able to focus on her studies, as grade 12 final exams are looming. Not a good time for disruptions from normalcy, such as it was.

Thanks again to all of you for your continued prayers and support.

June 7: A lot transpired today.

I think the turning point was when someone pointed out to Cassidy that the breath test apparatus was wrongly assembled, which negated any efforts she made. Once fixed, she was indeed able to have some tangible effect on it, which lightened her mood considerably, and possibly even made her more hopeful.

After this, her oxygen levels increased. And when we removed the oxygen altogether for a number of hours, they stayed within an acceptable range! Her coughing hasn't improved a whole lot, but her heart rate and blood pressure have stabilized. Good news!

There are still some troubling test results that need to be explained, however, and the x-rays taken today did not answer those questions. So more tests seem to be in her future. Tomorrow morning she will be going for a (severely modified) pulmonary function test, to give a clearer picture on what is actually happening to the lungs when she is inhaling and exhaling.

June 8: Good day, all!

And it was, in bits and pieces anyway. Cassidy did not rest well last night, due to a monitor beeping every time her breathing or heart rate was a little different. These beeps were not bad, however, in that they actually alerted us to the fact that her oxygen stayed in a good range and her heart rate was that of a very healthy person! Last night she was on oxygen. Tonight, however, she is trying to sleep without it, and so far her oxygen saturation rate is holding steady at 93 percent—which is fantastic!

So that's the good news. There's also talk of having her home by the weekend, which would be wonderful—but we've learned not to get too excited too soon.

Which is likely a good thing. There does seem to be something more chronic than the pneumonia at work here, and though she's had some testing done to help determine exactly what it may be, the results are somewhat skewed due to the existing pneumonia. So we may not know anything conclusively until this current infection has completely resolved. More tests and more patience seem to be the common prescriptions here!

Thanks for the continued prayers and support. They provide great comfort and strength.

June 9: Cassidy had a good day, with a visit from a friend from the Ronald McDonald House, a good haul of loot won at bingo, time with a wonderful volunteer playing games, and a nap during the second period of the Stanley Cup final game (not sure how she managed to sleep, when most other spectators were suffering from high blood pressure). Her breathing is also improved, though she still has a nasty cough to contend with.

Test results show no viral infection, so Cassidy was taken off isolation today. She will have a series of blood tests tomorrow, as well as another chest x-ray. So far, we have few answers, except that the acute pneumonia appears to be resolving. Praise God! The remaining issues will take time and patience to ascertain what else may be going on in her lungs, but the plan at present is for her to return home by the weekend, with a follow-up visit on Tuesday.

June 10: Today Cassidy woke up to a team of people wanting to take her blood—and I know stories about vampires are in vogue right now, but she was none too impressed! Great start to the day. Then she had a chest x-ray, and shortly thereafter Dave showed up so I could go home and attend Kali's choir and band concert. Nice break for me, and it looks as though Cassidy will be coming home tomorrow, so Dave won't need to stay more than just tonight. Good all around!

Then this evening, just as Kali and I were going to leave for the concert (which was great, by the way, and made me so proud of my daughter and her musical gifts!), Cassidy called. She was given a pass to leave the hospital for a few hours tonight, and just as Dave and she were driving to a fast-food joint, the car was rear-ended! So her pass was spent at the police station, filing an accident report! Thankfully she and Dave are fine, but my sweet little car is going to need some serious surgery on its back end! The bumper is severely crunched, and the hatch is no longer usable. Good thing the other guy's insurance is going to have to cover this boo-boo! Don't know quite how Dave is going to manage packing all Cassidy's luggage without the hatch, though. Should be interesting...

On the medical front, Cassidy's pneumonia seems to be

resolving, and tomorrow morning she will get her last IV dose of antibiotics, but will be on oral ones at home for quite some time. The docs are also concerned that there may be GVHD (hate those letters!) in the lungs, so she's going to be back on high-dose steroids for a while. She'll also be going for more pulmonary function tests (her least favourite) regularly and will have a CT scan of her lungs sometime in the next couple of weeks, after the pneumonia has completely resolved. But...the good news is she'll be coming home, and what was feared to become another lengthy stay in Calgary will be seen as just another one of those pesky and frightening speed bumps.

Please keep praying, because there's still a long road ahead for her.

June 12: We're all here in Lethbridge. And at this point our car is in worse shape than Cassidy is—count that as a blessing! She has to be back in Calgary on Tuesday for her regular checkup and has a bunch more meds to take every day, but her pneumonia is clearing up nicely! Good weekend so far!

June 16: Yesterday had Dave and Cassidy making their way to Calgary yet again. She had a clinic appointment at 9:15 a.m., which ended up being later, but the doctor was impressed with her recovery so far. Her blood chemistry levels were all in the normal range (praise the Lord!), a test showed a hint of mononucleosis (about which they are not at all concerned), and her pulmonary function test from earlier this week showed slight improvement from the last taken here in Lethbridge. All good news! There is definitely some GVHD present in her lungs, however, so next Tuesday Cassidy and I will be going to the Alberta Children's Hospital once again, this time for both a checkup and for a CT scan of her lungs. In the meantime she is on high-dose steroids and eating a lot! Not a bad thing in her case!

It has now been over two years since this increasingly significant journey began. Cassidy, who celebrated her six-teenth birthday on the 3rd of August, 2010, remains at home. However, with prednisone and immunosuppressants taken daily, she is still greatly limited as to the activities in which she is allowed to participate. The greatest disappoint-ment in this regard was the inability to go to the pool in the summer—her usual and favourite summer pastime. However, she was able to get together with friends, go on occasional outings, and spend time doing some of her favourite activities, so all in all, things could have been much worse. The GVHD in her lungs and liver seem to have stabilized, and that is a lot to be thankful for!

Cassidy is attempting a return to school this fall, and though we do not know how exactly this will turn out for her, God will guide us, and I therefore trust she will be blessed and live the life she was meant to. It just may not be what we thought we wanted for her.

Kali graduated from high school this June, made a public profession of her faith, and is attending The King's University College in Edmonton, where she plans to earn her bachelor of education degree. She has accomplished and been blessed with much, especially considering the choices she could have easily made when coping with the family circumstances. For this I am incredibly grateful to God and proud of my girl. She's had an oftentimes lonely and painful journey but always put on a smile and a brave face, putting one foot in front of the other and doing what needed to be done. It was extraordinarily difficult to

Kali with Mikey

see her leave home at the end of August, but she needs to find her own way and enjoy some frivolity.

Dave continues to work hard supporting the family, an increased burden as I was unemployed for a year and a half. He enjoys his job in construction, though, and finds it rewarding. Hopefully that eases his load somewhat—there's not much worse than hating your job, so I thank God he has been blessed with work that is challenging and enjoyable. He took good care of Kali and things on the home front during my absence, which relieved my burden and concerns considerably. He has also reached the end of a four-year term as an elder in our church and, I believe, is looking forward to once again being a regular congregant. He was blessed by the work he did, but it added stress to his life, and a break is welcome. He's also been blessed with incredibly supportive family and friends and likely would not have survived this well without them. I thank God for all these blessings.

As for me, I live and view life differently. I plan less and

Cassidy (left), Dave, Kali and Sonya with the Stanley Cup—won by a relative's team!

wait more. I speak less and listen more. I judge less and try to love more. I'm calmer, less likely to react impulsively, more introspective. And this is in large part due to very special people God has put in my life along the way. I also know that every person has their own set of trials, and though many of ours were and are very visible and public, one cannot assume to know what is going on in another's life nor presume to know how they should respond and react to either blessings or adversity.

Over the past several months that I have been back in Lethbridge, I have been blessed to be working with my pastor, first on getting a book he had written ready for publication, then with the distribution of it, and now with this more personal project. This book was his idea, bred from the fact that through his own illness, he was able to better understand and empathize with Cassidy's. This in and of itself is evidence of how God is always good, and I am most grateful.

I have returned to my job as an educational assistant on a part-time basis, something I had mixed feelings about. However, God placed the opportunity in my path, and a second income will relieve some of Dave's burden, so I will take it on as another adventure and be blessed by it, too, I am sure. I will also be, for the first time, taking on the office of deaconess in our church. I am sure this will present challenges and rewards, and I anticipate both.

What does the future hold? I do not know. None of us knows. We can plan and dream, and it is important to put one foot in front of the other and do our best at what we endeavour to do, but the future really is out of our control. Though it has been a hard lesson to learn, letting go and truly letting God take control is incredibly freeing and comforting. This I know for sure:

> God is doing a greater work in us, and that can only come as we learn to trust him no matter how dark the days and sleepless the nights. And it is only as we have been through the darkness with him that what we know with our heads slides down into our hearts, and our hearts no longer demand answers. The 'Why?' becomes unimportant when we believe that God can and will redeem the pain for our good and his glory…. When I put the sovereignty of God beside his unfailing love, my heart can rest. —Verdell Davis.[9]

And, more importantly, from Romans 8:

> *And we know that for those who love God all things work together for good, for those who are called according to his purpose…For I am sure that neither death nor life, nor angels nor rulers, nor things present nor things to come, nor powers, nor height nor*

depth, nor anything else in all creation, will be able to separate us from the love of God in Christ Jesus our Lord (Romans 8:28-39).

What beautiful and eternal comfort, in what can be a less than beautiful and very temporal life. And to this my response is gratitude. For God is always good.

CONCLUSION

This has been Cassidy's story, as told by her mother. But we also asked Cassidy herself to comment on her experience. Here are her answers to questions we posed:

1. What has changed in how you view the world, your beliefs, your relationship with God?
I now view the world in a different light. I hate it when people complain, argue with their friends, and don't do what they're asked to do, like chores. I view the world as a place where they should go through what I, and my family, have gone through—have that pain, sadness, or that scare—and then see if they will argue, or complain about school or chores. I want to yell at them and say "Suck it up; you don't such have a bad life!" It has given me a different insight into the world. I used to argue with my friends, and now I see it as a waste of time, and life's too short to spend it arguing and complaining; I used to hate school, and now I love it. I (try to) do as I am told.

2. Were you/are you mad at God? How did/do you deal with that?
I was, and sometimes still am, mad at God. I cry and I pray that it would all go away. It's really frustrating that I can't eat some fast food, drink soft drinks, have a burger straight from A&W with lettuce and tomato; go to restaurants, stores,

farms, dog pounds; get a job, etc., because of my immuno-suppression. I was mad because God chose me for suffering and that my life became worse off than my original problem (severe chronic neutropenia). I don't remember much of what happened: the pain, how long it was, when things happened, if I was scared or not, if I thought I was going to die; I don't remember (chemo brain).

3. Do you believe God sent these trials to you? If so, what purpose do you see in them?
I believe these trials were given to me for a reason—so I can change my life, influence other people, and maybe some things will come out of it that I don't see yet.

4. How have you come to peace about this?
I came to peace about this by getting as far as I have. The worst part is over (I hope), and I'm almost healed. I have learned that I should live day to day as best as I can (leave the arguing and complaining to other people).

Here also are some further reflections from Sonya:

One of the most difficult parts of this journey has been the fact that Cassidy's suffering isn't the only suffering to contend with. So many children and families have become part of our life, albeit briefly, whether in the hospital or at the Ronald McDonald House. We have seen children as young as newborn and as old as seventeen or eighteen face devastating trials—prematurity, birth defects, injuries, cancer, and other illnesses and diseases. I have become close to many families and shared my own pain and fears whilst they shared theirs. And though we have seen many children return home relatively healthy and strong, so many were not offered that privilege. It is mind-numbing and heartbreaking to think of the children we have loved and lost. So senseless to my limited mind. So painful to my human heart.

At the time I write this, I've known, over the past two years, fifteen children who have died. Have known their families, their journeys through battles no child should have to fight. I have seen them live, and die. And each one again breaks my heart to the point where I almost want to become a hermit, never meet another person, never again let my heart feel love—because then it will no longer feel loss. And there are times I have done exactly that, tried to numb myself to the lives of those surrounding me, but they always find their way back in, and I know, somehow, for some reason beyond my understanding, that this is part of my journey, part of what is shaping and forming me.

And though I despise the diseases, hate the suffering life is too often full of, and hate that the devil still has his way with us here on earth, I know that God is in control...over all things...and that everything—everything—has a purpose. Some may ask, and I judge them not for asking, how can God allow or permit such innocent children to suffer so? I have asked the same question myself...and I have no answer. But I do know that he works his purpose out in each of us, through all our joys and all our trials, and though his ways are mysterious to me, that mystery also offers me comfort. Because if I, in my limited intelligence, could fully understand him, he would not be God but just another weak, imperfect, limited being. So I look back, see all he has done, see the ways he has guided my life—against my will, often—all for my good. And so I choose to trust him and know him, knowing that he does love me, knowing that he wants all that is good for me, knowing that that may not be my experience here on earth, but also knowing that my time here is short—minuscule—and that there is an eternity for me to live once my existence here has passed. And it is for that that he is preparing me, and for that he is preparing all of us. It is up to us to see it, to grasp it, to embrace it, and to trust him.

Cassidy is doing relatively well at present, although still not fully recovered. For myself (Cameron), I am in remission and will (DV) have been back to full-time ministry for two

2010—A healthy Cameron with his family:
Matt (left), Margaret, James

years by the time this is published. But what if the results had been different than they are at present? What if Cassidy had not survived her treatments, which seemed a very real possibility at times? What if I were writing as a dying man with only months to live? Would I still be able to say that God is always good? How can I say that to those whose diagnosis and future outlook is more bleak than my own?

I have found that even among some Christians, one response to catastrophic suffering in their lives is anger with God, as if somehow they deserved better. They ask "Why me?" rather than "Why not me?" The same cry of pain can also be heard in Scripture, especially the psalms. Yet, as Jerry Bridges points out in his book *Trusting God Even When Life Hurts*, we need to distinguish between asking *why* as a spontaneous cry of anguish, which is a natural human reaction, and asking *why* as a persistent and demanding accusation, which is a sinful human reaction.

> Three of the psalms begin with *why*: "Why...do you stand far off?" "Why have you forsaken me?" "Why have you rejected us forever?" (Psalms 10, 22, 74). But each of those psalms ends on a note of trust in God. The psalm writers did not allow their *whys* to drag on. They did not allow them to take root and grow into accusations against God. Their *whys* were really cries of anguish, a natural reaction to pain.[10]

This is an important distinction. God is more than capable of handling our emotions, and he understands our pain. On the other hand, to engage in persistent and demanding accusations against the providence of God is to demonstrate a profound misunderstanding, that God is being unfair, when in fact if God were to be strictly fair with us, we would all be in hell. Anything short of that is grace.

Another common misunderstanding among Christians is the belief that all suffering in our lives is sent by Satan and not by God. In this way, they try to preserve their faith in the goodness of God. But this simply will not stand the test of Scripture. The classic text here is the book of Job. To be sure, Satan is the one who afflicts Job, but on each occasion it is clear that this is only because God permits him to. It is God who initially presents Satan with the challenge, "*Have you considered my servant Job...?*" Satan responds, "*Does Job fear God for no reason?*" (In other words, Satan accuses Job of only serving God because he has been so blessed by him.) Satan continues, "*But stretch out your hand and touch all that he has, and he will curse you to your face.*" The Lord responds, "*Behold, all that he has is in your hands*" (see Job 1:8-12).

Notice that Job's possessions, his children, and ultimately Job himself were placed in Satan's hands to do with as he wished. But Satan recognized that in reality this was possible only because God had stretched out *his* hand and allowed all these evils to befall Job. Without God's permission, Satan could have *done* nothing. As Joni Eareckson Tada says in another context, "I don't care if you use permit, allow, or ordained; it's all the same thing. Ultimately, it goes back to God being in charge. I don't think there is a real difference.[11]

A number of years ago, a Jewish rabbi in New York, Harold Kushner, wrote a best-selling book called *When Bad Things Happen to Good People*. In this book, Kushner tackles the age-old problem of how God can be both all powerful and perfectly good. This is how he resolves it:

Let me suggest that the author of the Book of Job takes the position which neither Job nor his friends take. He believes in God's goodness and in Job's goodness, and is prepared to give up his belief...that God is all-powerful. Bad things do happen to good people in this world, but it is not God who wills it. God would like people to get what they deserve in life, but He cannot always arrange it. Forced to choose between a good God who is not totally powerful, or a powerful God who is not totally good, the author of the Book of Job chooses to believe in God's goodness.[12]

What is particularly troubling about Kushner's position is that one hears modifications of it in Christian circles. There is even a popular movement known as "Open Theism," held by some prominent evangelicals, which postulates that God doesn't know the future and so can't be held responsible for the tragic things that come our way. He didn't cause them, he deliberately limited his power in such a way that he couldn't prevent them, and so he really does sympathize with us as one who shares our pain but didn't cause it. The appeal of this is obvious, but the implications are devastating. If God isn't in total control all of the time, if he doesn't know the future, how can we possibly take comfort from the assurance that he will cause all things to work together for our good?

Jesus said that our heavenly Father's control is so extensive that not a sparrow falls to the ground apart from his will and there's not a hair on our heads he hasn't counted (Matthew 10:29,30). We like that, because he also tells us we're of much more value than many sparrows, so if he watches out for sparrows, how much more does he watch out for us? That makes us feel good. But the same God, in order to make a point to his prophet Jonah, sent a worm to chew up a vine that was providing shade for Jonah (Jonah 4:5-11).

God says in Isaiah 45:7, "*I form the light and create darkness, I make well-being and create calamity; I am the LORD, who does all these things.*" He asks rhetorically in Amos 3:6, "*When disaster comes to a city, has not the LORD caused it?*" (NIV). The story of Joseph and his brothers makes it clear that what the brothers intended for harm, God intended for good (Genesis 50:20). The same principle was at work most especially in the death of God's own Son who was "*handed over to you by God's set purpose and foreknowledge*" to be put to death by "*wicked men*" (Acts 2:23, NIV, cf. 4:27-28).

There is profound mystery here, but it is precisely because God is in total control of evil as well as good that, even when we don't understand his purposes, we can fall back on that promise with which the introduction to this book began: "*And we know that for those who love God all things work together for good, for those who are called according to his purpose*" (Romans 8:28). When we read on we find that his purpose began with his eternal plan, and it ends in our glorification. And its focal point is that we might be "*conformed to the image of his Son.*" In other words, so that we might become like Jesus and go to be with him. Whatever it takes to accomplish this is good!

One of the most powerful reminders of this is an article by well-known pastor and author John Piper called "Don't Waste Your Cancer."[13] Piper wrote the article in 2006, when he was diagnosed with prostate cancer. David Powlison of the Christian Counseling and Education Foundation, who received the same diagnosis close to the same time, offers commentary on each point. The entire article is well worth reading and can be found on the desiringGod.org website. What I would like to do here is highlight five of Piper's points, without any commentary of my own except at the end:

1. You will waste your cancer if you do not believe it is designed for you by God.

It will not do to say that God only *uses* our cancer but does not design it. What God permits, he permits for a reason. And that reason is his design. If God foresees molecular developments becoming cancer, he can stop it or not. If he does not, he has a purpose. Since he is infinitely wise, it is right to call this purpose a design. Satan is real and causes many pleasures and pains. But he is not ultimate. So when he strikes Job with boils (Job 2:7), Job attributes it ultimately to God (2:10) and the inspired writer agrees: "They...comforted him for all the evil that the Lord had brought upon him" (Job 42:11). If you don't believe your cancer is designed for you by God, you will waste it.

2. You will waste your cancer if you believe it is a curse and not a gift.

"There is therefore now no condemnation for those who are in Christ Jesus" (Romans 8:1). "Christ redeemed us from the curse of the law by becoming a curse for us" (Galatians 3:13). "There is no enchantment against Jacob, no divination against Israel" (Numbers 23:23). "The Lord God is a sun and shield; the Lord bestows favor and honor. No good thing does he withhold from those who walk uprightly" (Psalm 84:11).

4. You will waste your cancer if you refuse to think about death.

We will all die, if Jesus postpones his return. Not to think about what it will be like to leave this life and meet God is folly. Ecclesiastes 7:2 says, "It is better to go to the house of mourning [a funeral] than to go to the house of feasting, for this is the end of all mankind, and the living will lay it to heart." How can you lay it to heart if you won't think about it? Psalm 90:12 says, "Teach us to number our days that we may get a heart of wisdom." Numbering your days means thinking about how few there are and that they will end. How will you get a heart of wisdom if you refuse to think about this? What a waste, if we do not think about death.

5. You will waste your cancer if you think that "beating" cancer means staying alive rather than cherishing Christ.

Satan's and God's designs in your cancer are not the same. Satan designs to destroy your love for Christ. God designs to deepen your love for Christ. Cancer does not win if you die. It wins if you fail to cherish Christ. God's design is to wean you off the breast of the world and feast you on the sufficiency of Christ. It is meant to help you say and feel, "I count everything as loss because of the surpassing worth of knowing Christ Jesus my Lord." And to know that therefore, "To live is Christ, and to die is gain" (Philippians 3:8; 1:21).

9. You will waste your cancer if you treat sin as casually as before.

Are your besetting sins as attractive as they were before you had cancer? If so you are wasting your cancer. Cancer is designed to destroy the appetite for sin. Pride, greed, lust, hatred, unforgiveness, impatience, laziness, procrastination—all these are the adversaries that cancer is meant to attack. Don't just think of battling *against* cancer. Also think of battling *with* cancer. All these things are worse enemies than cancer. Don't waste the power of cancer to crush these foes. Let the presence of eternity make the sins of time look as futile as they really are. "What does it profit a man if he gains the whole world and loses or forfeits himself?" (Luke 9:25).

Joni Eareckson (now Eareckson Tada) and Steve Estes make a similar point in *A Step Further*:

When God brings suffering into your life as a Christian, be it mild or drastic, He is forcing you to decide on issues you have been avoiding. He is pressing you to ask yourself some questions: Am I going to continue trying to live in two worlds, obeying Christ and my own sinful desires? Or am I going to refuse to worry? Am I going to be grateful in trials? Am I going to abandon my sins? In short, am I going to be like Christ? He provides the suffering, but the choice is yours.[14]

Eareckson and Estes are reflecting on her (Joni's) paralysis as a young woman. Piper is writing about cancer, but the points made really apply to any form of suffering that helps us focus on what really matters in life. If we really believe that the greatest blessing of all is to love Jesus, to become like him, to know that he is always with us and that one day we shall go to be with him, then whatever it takes in this life to get us to that point is more than worth it. We can be sure of this, because God is always good!

MEDICAL TERM GLOSSARY

acute myelogenous leukemia: a cancer of the myeloid line of blood cells, characterized by the rapid growth of abnormal white blood cells that accumulate in the bone marrow and interfere with the production of normal blood cells

adenovirus: commonly causes illness of the respiratory system; however, it may also cause various other illnesses, such as gastroenteritis, conjunctivitis, cystitis, and rash illness. Patients with compromised immune systems are especially susceptible to severe complications of adenovirus infection.

adult mesenchymal stem cells (MSCs): cells from an adult donor that can develop into distinct tissue such as bone; tendons; muscles; adipose tissue; cartilage; nerve tissue; and blood and blood vessels

albumin: the main protein of plasma

allogeneic stem cell transplant: a stem cells transplant using stem cells from an unrelated donor

anaphylactic reaction: a rapidly progressing, life-threatening allergic reaction

aneurism: localized widening (dilatation) of an artery, vein, or the heart. At the area of an aneurysm, there is typically a bulge and the wall is weakened and may rupture.

antiviral: an agent that kills a virus or that suppresses its ability to multiply and reproduce

asthma: chronic (long-lasting) inflammatory disease of the airways

autologous stem cell transplant: a transplant using the stem cells from one's own blood or bone marrow

Benadryl: an antihistamine for the temporary relief of allergy symptoms

biopsy: the removal and examination of a sample of tissue from a living body for diagnostic purposes

bone marrow biopsy: a procedure in which cellular material is removed from the pelvis or breastbone and examined under a microscope to look for the presence of abnormal blood cells

Broviac: a catheter (tube) that is passed through a large vein in the neck and is used to administer medications and chemotherapy and to access blood for testing

central line: IV tubing inserted for continuous access to a central vein for administering fluids and medicines and for obtaining diagnostic information (Broviac or PICC)

chemotherapy: chemicals used to kill cells, usually cancerous cells

contrast: x-ray dyes infused to provide contrast, for example, between blood vessels and other tissue

Crohn's: an inflammatory disease that mainly affects the intestines

CT scan: x-ray images taken by a computer that creates cross-sectional views of the anatomy

dermatologist: a doctor who diagnoses and treats skin problems

eczema: a topical inflammation of the skin

endoscopy: an examination of the inside of the body using a flexible, lighted instrument

enzymes: Proteins that are a significant factor in specific chemical reactions in the body

gastrointestinal (GI): mouth, esophagus, stomach, small and large intestines, pancreas, liver, and gallbladder

graft versus host disease (GVHD): a reaction of donated bone marrow or stem cells against a patient's own tissue

grafting: when the body accepts donor cells as its own

granulocyte-colony stimulating factor (G-CSF): a factor that stimulates the production of neutrophils (a type of white cell)

Gravol: an anti-nausea medication

H1N1: A virus responsible for a flu pandemic in 2009 that was originally referred to as "swine flu"

haematologist: a doctor who specializes in the diagnosis, treatment and prevention of diseases of the blood and bone marrow

haemoglobin: the oxygen-carrying and predominant protein in red blood cells

heparin lock: an agent used to prevent blood clots in lumens between uses

immunosuppressant: an agent that suppresses an immune response, often used to prevent rejection of transplanted tissue

intravenous (IV): literally "into a vein"

Kostmann's syndrome: severe chronic congenital neutropenia

lethargic: a state of abnormal drowsiness

lipid: fats that are an important part of living cells

lumen: entry-point into a central line catheter (Broviac or PICC)

lymphoma: a tumour within the lymphatic system (the part of the body that helps protect itself from bacteria and other foreign matter)

mononucleosis: a viral infection

monosomy 7: the complete or partial loss of the seventh chromosome

morphine: a powerful painkiller

mucositis: inflammation of the mucous membranes of the digestive tract

mutation: a permanent structural change in the DNA or RNA

neutrophils: white blood cells that combat bacterial and fungal infections

NG tube: a tube that is passed through the nose into the stomach

oncologist: a doctor who specializes in the diagnosis, treatment, and prevention of cancer

oncology: the field of medicine devoted to cancer

Ondansetron: an anti-nausea medication

Osiris Therapeutics, Inc.: self-described as "a leading stem cell company focused on developing and marketing products to treat medical conditions in the inflammatory, autoimmune, orthopedic and cardiovascular areas"

paediatrician: a doctor specializing in the health and development of children

parasite: an organism that lives in or on and takes its nourishment from another organism

PET scan, "Positron Emission Tomography": a highly specialized imaging technique that uses short-lived radioactive substances to produce three-dimensional coloured images of those substances functioning within the body

PICC line: a **"Peripherally Inserted Central Catheter"** is a surgically implanted form of intravenous access that can be used for a prolonged period of time.

pneumonia: inflammation of one or both lungs

prednisone: a synthetic steroid drug that is particularly effective as an immunosuppressant drug and is often used to treat certain inflammatory diseases

pulmonary function test: a test designed to measure how well the lungs are working

radiation: use of energy rays to treat disease

severe chronic neutropenia (congenital): a very rare (650 cases worldwide) genetic disorder of the bone marrow characterized by a lack of neutrophils evident at birth, making the sufferer highly susceptible to bacterial and fungal infections

spinal tap: a procedure where spinal fluid is removed from the spinal canal for the purpose of diagnostic testing

spleen: an organ located in the upper left part of the abdomen near the stomach. The spleen produces lymphocytes; it is the largest lymphatic organ in the body. The spleen also filters the blood, serves as a major reservoir for blood and destroys blood cells that are aged.

tonsils: small masses of lymphoid tissue at the back of the throat, which commonly become inflamed and/or infected. Chronic or recurrent inflammation may necessitate surgical removal of the tonsils (tonsillectomy). Tonsils are a first-line of defence against infection, so their removal in Cassidy's case was significant.

TPN: "Total Parenteral Nutrition" provides a patient with all of the fluid and the essential nutrients through an IV when they are unable to feed themselves by mouth.

ultrasound: high-frequency sound waves used to create pictures of soft tissues and body cavities

ENDNOTES

[1] The person who loaned me the book, Susanne Hummel, was herself subsequently diagnosed with the same kind of lymphoma I had, except hers was on the neck. Other members of the congregation who developed various types of cancer both during and especially after my illness include Geert Procee (later deceased from a stroke), Bill Biesbroek (deceased), Lena Boutestein (deceased), and Jessiann Bosch. Rosemary Konynenbelt, who was being treated for a tumour on her brain when I began my ministry in Lethbridge, made a good recovery but more recently suffered an aneurism, from which she continues to recover. Other members had experiences with cancer prior to my arrival, and one, Anne Bosma, passed away from liver cancer not long after I came. Ministry to these individuals and their families has been a special blessing.

[2] Ajith Fernando, "To Serve Is to Suffer," *Christianity Today*, August 2010, 33.

[3] C.S. Lewis, *The Problem of Pain* (New York: Macmillan, 1969), 93.

[4] C. John Miller, *The Heart of a Servant Leader: Letters from Jack Miller*, ed. Barbara Miller Juliani (Phillipsburg, NJ: P & R Publishing, 2004), 293-294.

[5] At that time, we lived in Iron Springs, a thirty-minute drive north of Lethbridge. We moved to Lethbridge in 2003.

[6] Matthias; copyright inspiring-quotes-and-stories.com-2006.

[7] Corrie Ten Boom quoted in *Scaring: Webster's Quotations, Facts and Phrases* (ICON Group International, Inc., 2008), 2.

[8] Joni Eareckson Tada, reading for August 5, in *Pearls of Great Price: 366 Daily Devotional Readings* (Grand Rapids: Zondervan, 2006).

[9] Verdell Davis, *Let Me Grieve But Not Forever: A Journey Out of the Darkness of Loss* (Nashville, Tenn.: 1994), 76.

[10] Jerry Bridges, *Trusting God Even when Life Hurts* (Colorado Springs: NavPress, 1988), 124.

[11] Joni Eareckson Tada, "Something Greater Than Healing," *Christianity Today*, October 2010, 32.

[12] Harold Kushner, *When Bad Things Happen to Good People* (New York: Random House, Inc. 1981), 42.

[13] The article was also published as an appendix in John Piper and Justin Taylor, eds., *Suffering and the Sovereignty of God* (Wheaton, Ill: Crossway Books, 2006). I am indebted to Marian Aarsen for drawing my attention to it. Marian is a member of my congregation who was diagnosed with pancreatic cancer and then discovered that the diagnosis was mistaken! Her brush with cancer, however, had a profound effect on her.

[14] Joni Eareckson and Steve Estes, A *Step Further* (Grand Rapids: Zondervan, 1980), 77. Joni, who first became known as a result of her account of becoming paralyzed from a diving accident, as told in her book *Joni,* was recently diag-

nosed with breast cancer. She had just written *A Place for Healing: Wrestling with the Mystery of Suffering, Pain and God's Sovereignty* and comments on it on her blog (October 5th, 2010, www.joniandfriends.org/blog/tuesday-oct-5th-update-joni/): "Normally I don't talk a lot about my books on this blog, but I'm thinking twice. No book has caused quite the stir as my recent one, *A Place of Healing*. The day it went to press I learned I had cancer—I scrambled to amend the epilogue, and then the next afternoon I was in surgery. I've flipped through its pages lately, wondering if I'd change anything (like, Joni, you shouldn't be shooting so fast from your hip with those Bible verses). But I've been pleasantly surprised. Although I was writing about chronic pain, I've found some powerful 'aha' moments that have blessed me through this cancer."